DEVOTIONAL STUDY GUIDE

Unshakable HOPE

BUILDING OUR LIVES ON THE PROMISES OF GOD

MAX LUCADO

TRILOGY
CHRISTIAN
PUBLISHING

TRILOGY
CHRISTIAN
PUBLISHING

Trilogy Christian Publishers
A Wholly Owned Subsidiary of Trinity Broadcasting Network
2442 Michelle Drive
Tustin, CA 92780

For information about special discounts for bulk purchases, please contact Trilogy Christian Publishing.

Design, Diane Whisner
Cover image, Getty Images. Photographer, Roy Morsch

Manufactured in the United States of America

10 9 8 7 6 5 4 3 2 1

Library of Congress Cataloging-in-Publication Data is available.

ISBN 978-1-6408-8903-3
ISBN 978-1-6408-8906-4 (ebook)

Unshakable
HOPE

Contents

CONTENTS

UNSHAKABLE HOPE

INTRODUCTION

They do not build things like they used to. Cathedrals, castles, and monuments still stand centuries after they were constructed. From the cathedrals of Rome to the Alamo near my own home, there is something special about a building that stands the test of time. Wars could not destroy them. Storms could not devastate them. You might even say they are unshakable.

I wonder what kind of life are you building? We live in a shaky world. Promises break. Stock markets crash. Relationships crumble. The pillars of our faith will be tested. Do you want to be unshakable in a shaky world? You can build your life on the enduring promises of God. Do you have a problem? God has a promise. These promises stand the test of time, and they weather life's biggest storms. In this study, we are going to explore some of these great and precious promises found in God's Word. When the world rages around you, you can stand with Unshakable Hope.

MY DECLARATION:

I am building my life on the promises of God.
Because His promises are unbreakable, my world is unshakable. I
do not stand on the problems of life or the pain in life.
I stand on the great and precious promises of God.

CHAPTER ONE:

THE KNOWABLE GOD

One of my favorite childhood memories is greeting my father as he came home from work. My mother, who worked an evening shift at the hospital, would leave the house around three in the afternoon. Dad would arrive home at three-thirty. My brother and I were left alone for that half-hour with strict instructions not to leave the house until Dad arrived. Even if he were a little late, our confidence was unshaken that he would be coming through that door in a matter of time.

We would take our positions on the couch and watch cartoons, always keeping one ear alert to the driveway. Even the best "Daffy Duck" would be abandoned when we heard Dad's car.

I can remember running out to meet him and getting swept up in his big (often sweaty) arms. As he carried me toward the house, he would put his big-brimmed straw hat on my head, and for a moment I would be a cowboy. We would sit on the porch as he removed his oily work boots (which were never allowed in the house). As he took them off I would pull them on, and for a moment I would be a wrangler. Then we would go indoors and open his lunch pail. Any leftover snacks, which he always seemed to have, were for my brother and me to split. It was great. Boots, hats, and snacks. What more could a five-year-old want?

But suppose that is all I got. Suppose my dad, rather than coming home, just sent some things home. Boots for me to play in. A hat for me to wear. Snacks for me to eat. Would that be enough? Maybe so, but not for long. Soon the gifts would lose their charm. Soon, if not immediately, I would ask, "Where is Dad?"

Or consider something worse. Suppose he called me up and said, "Max, I won't be coming home anymore. But I will send my boots and hat over, and every afternoon you can play in them."

No deal. That wouldn't work. Even a five-year-old knows it is the person, not the presents, which makes a reunion special. It is not the frills—it is the father.

Perhaps you had a father like that. A father who, for whatever reason, by circumstance or decision, was not present for birthdays, holidays, or graduations. Perhaps a gift or card on those special days was the only connection you had with him. Or maybe not even that. No cards, no contact. Your father was completely absent. The idea of a father involved in the everyday details of your life is a foreign concept to you. And yet, in our hearts, we know this was never the way it was meant to be. We were meant to be in relationship.

Now, imagine God making us this offer: *I will give you anything you desire. Anything. Perfect love. Eternal peace. You will never be afraid or alone. No confusion will enter your mind. No anxiety or boredom will enter your heart. You will never lack for anything. There will be no sin. No guilt. No rules. No expectations. No failure. You will never be lonely. You will never hurt. You will never die. But there is one catch—*

You will never see my face.

Would you want it? No? Neither would I. Neither does God. The truth is this—He wants us to know Him. In fact, He promises we can know Him.

"I promise" is such a simple, powerful phrase. No frills. No colorful adjectives. Yet, it locks the sentences that come before or after it into an unbreakable commitment. But for many of us, the idea of a promise hasn't meant much. We have seen promises just as easily broken as made. And just as easily forgotten as remembered. But not with God. When He makes a promise, He does not pick the lock, cut it, or swap it out with a magician's fake. He throws away the key. His promises cannot be undone and will not be broken.

Look up this beautiful promise from God in Hebrews 8:11 (NIV):

No longer will they teach their neighbor, or say to one another, _____, because they will all _____, from the least to the greatest.

Some years ago Denalyn and I went on a tour of the Eiffel Tower in Paris. It is a fascinating iconic structure, towering high above the great City of Lights. Some tourists wore headphones that provided a self-paced tour. Others followed guides and listened at different junctures. Others did not have headphones and did not have a tour guide. They mistakenly assumed they could answer all their questions on their own. That was me. I soon regretted not having the assistance of a headset or tour guide. I had more questions than I had answers. How long did it take to build? Who had the idea to build it? Why this location? Has the building ever been struck by lightning?

Denalyn did not know. I did not know. But the guides knew. So, I will confess, I eavesdropped. I heard a lot, but what I did *not* hear was this invitation:

"Would any of you like to get to know the designer?" Or, "Could I interest anyone in a relationship with the architect?"

Such offers were never made. Why? Well, for one thing, the designer is dead. He no longer inhabits the earth. But even if Gustave Eiffel were still alive, what are the odds that he would make himself available to be known? To receive inquiries? To personally entertain questions? No, we cannot know the designer of the Eiffel Tower.

But we can know the Designer of the Grand Canyon, the human eye, and the Milky Way Galaxy. The architect of the Empire State building is dead, buried, and unavailable. But the One who furrowed the Malvern Canyon in the seabed of the Atlantic Ocean is not. The creator of the Eiffel Tower building can no longer speak, but the Creator of Mt. Everest is alive and well. And He invites us to know Him.

Look again at this great promise.

"They will all _____ me" (Hebrews 8:11).

GOD'S PROMISE:

He wants to know us and promises to make Himself known to us.

That is God's Word to us. We can rest in it. But we can also act on it. God's promises propel us to new depths in our relationship with Him. Here is how we can answer His invitation to know Him:

> ## MY PROMISE:
>
> *I will make the knowledge of God my highest pursuit.*

Like a resplendent gem, turning to reveal new beauty at every angle, there are so many things to learn about God. Throughout history, He has continued to reveal different facets of who He is to His people. And for all eternity we will continue to discover more. But there are some things that we know to be true now.

God envisions a day and even guarantees the moment when all who want to know Him will do so. What a difference this promise makes. People of the Promise make it their highest aim to know God. They believe that the day is coming when they will see Him face to face. The mysteries will be solved. The majesty will be witnessed. Even now, God is pulling back the curtain, inviting us to take a glimpse.

He begins with this foundational truth: **God is.**

God is the Alpha and Omega. The beginning and the end. He was before all things. And all things come from Him. Everything that exists gives evidence of God's existence. The intricacy of the snowflake, the roar of a thunderstorm, the precision of the honeybee, the bubbling of a cool mountain stream. These miracles and a million more give testimony to the existence of a brilliant, wise, and tireless God.

To deny the existence of God, after all He has done and all we can see, is an atrocious, disastrous choice. God gives no quarter to those who, upon seeing what God has done, dare to announce that He does not exist. David pens the first line of Psalm 14 with this warning, "The fool says in his heart, 'There is no God.'"

Suppose you prepared a delicious meal and invited guests to your table. Imagine that one of the guests, upon eating the food, was to wipe his mouth with a napkin and announce: "What good fortune this meal is. All the ingredients tumbled out of the cabinet onto your preparation table. They intermingled at precisely the correct measurement. What a wonder of science that they then elevated themselves up and into the oven where they cooked for the perfect amount of time at the appropriate temperature. The oven door then flew open with a bang and the food flew out onto the table for our consumption."

What would you, as the preparer of the meal, think of such an opinion? Mightn't you use the same language as the psalmist? Foolish.

The second truth is this: **God is knowable.**

He has not hidden Himself. He does not close the door to His children. He does not resist our questions or refuse our inquiries; just the opposite: He promises success to all who search for Him.

There are many things in life you may never understand. The periodic table of elements, the way of a woman with a man, the reason God made mosquitoes. Our Maker never guarantees that we will comprehend the cosmos or plumb the ocean depths. But when it comes to knowing God, God wants you to know that you can know Him.

This is the highest of God's promises. **We shall know God.** Scripture curates many pledges, but all fall beneath this one. Of the Bible's armada of covenants, this is the flagship.

And isn't knowing Him knowing all? The apostle Paul was quick to abandon all accomplishment if it meant he could, in his words:

_____ Him, and the power of His resurrection, and the _____ of His sufferings... (Philippians 3:10 NIV).

The goal of life, from God's perspective, is to know God. The reason each day dawns is to grant more time to know Him. The universe exists to declare His glory. The church exists to promote His beauty. The Scripture exists to reveal His heart. Even marriage is designed to teach us about a relationship with God. To know God is our highest pursuit.

You were made to know God. You were made to feel His grace pulse through your heart. You were made to stand on the edge of His wisdom and gaze with a gasp over the side. You were made to know God. You were made for more than paychecks, weekends, and a nice retirement. You were created for more than a simple, ordinary, mundane life.

Do not settle for mastering a skill; pursue the Master of the skies. Do not settle for a life well lived; explore the Maker of life himself. Do not settle for pleasures and possessions; aim to know the Person of heaven.

You were made to know Him. You are at your best when you pursue Him. Are you shaken by the struggles of life? Then ponder the strength of God. Are you disappointed with the pleasure of this earth? Then enlarge your scope to include the vastness of the Godhead, the mystery of the Trinity, and the beauty of the Cross. Would you like to lose your sorrow? Dispel your stress? Then dive headfirst into the immensity of God who has never not been and will never grow weary. Do you feel small and insignificant? Then lose yourself in the tender arms of your mighty heavenly Father; ponder His words of love. Make Him the cynosure of your life.

- The pursuit of money will make you greedy.
- The pursuit of pleasure will leave you empty.
- The pursuit of knowledge will puff you up.
- The pursuit of popularity will shut you out.

But the pursuit of God will satisfy your soul.

Why? This quest is your calling. You were made to know Him. God guarantees that those who seek Him will find Him. It is his promise. And we can build our lives upon this promise.

So make knowing God your highest pursuit. Jeremiah 9:23–24 (NIV) puts it this way:

This is what the LORD says: "Let not the wise boast of _____ or the strong boast of _____ or the rich boast of _____, but let the one who boasts boast about this: that they have the _____, that I am the LORD, who exercises kindness, justice and righteousness on earth, for in these I _____,"declares the LORD.

When it comes to knowledge of God, our finest thoughts are first grade math to His advanced algebra. God is incomprehensible, but that does not discourage us. Just the opposite! We will explore Him for eternity. In the age to come, we will enjoy an eternal adventure of discovery. God's attributes will fascinate us forever!

Put your hope firmly in God's promise to all of us:

"They will know Me."

He will make Himself known to all who seek Him. Make sure that you are one of them by starting with this promise of your own:

"I will make the knowledge of God my highest pursuit."

QUESTIONS FOR REFLECTION:

1. How would you describe the God you know?

_____

_____

_____

_____

2. How does God describe Himself? *(Exodus 34:5–7)*

_____

_____

_____

_____

3. What steps can you take to know God more today? This month? This year?

_____

_____

_____

_____

Chapter Two:

The God of Peace

It was a sunny day in July. Even in 1861, Washington, DC, was crowded and busy. A trip to the countryside would be nice. The thought of the picnickers does not surprise us. The people weren't the first or the last to pack a meal and set out for a Sunday afternoon excursion. No, it was not the picnic baskets that made this entourage notable. It is where they were going to unpack them.

They were going to a battlefield. The crowd rode horses and buggies to Manassas to witness their Union soldiers bring an end to what they considered to be a short rebellion. Their intent was to sit on blankets, eat their chicken, and cheer from a distance.

One soldier described them as a "throng of sightseers."

But it was not long before reality rushed in. The sound of gunfire, the sight of blood, and the screams of wounded soldiers. The people soon realized—this was no picnic. Fathers grabbed children and husbands called for their wives. They jumped into their wagons and onto their horses. Some were caught in a stampede of retreating Union troops. One spectator, a congressman from New York, strayed too close to the combat and was caught by Confederate soldiers. He spent six months in a Richmond prison.

That was the last time any onlookers took a picnic basket to a battlefield.

Or was it?

Could it be that we make the same mistake? Could it be that we are under the same false assumption? Is it possible that we do today what the Washingtonians did then? According to the Bible, there is a war a-raging.

Ephesians 6 puts it this way:

Our fight is not against _____ but against the rulers and authorities and the powers of this world's darkness, against the spiritual powers of evil in the heavenly world. That is why you need to put on _____. Then on the day of evil you will be able to stand strong. And when you have finished the whole fight, you will still be standing. So stand strong, with the _____ tied around your waist and the protection of right living on your chest. On your feet wear the _____ of peace to help you stand strong. And also use the _____ of faith with which you can stop all the burning arrows of the Evil One (Ephesians 6:12–16 NCV).

We are in a battle, and we must take it seriously. A battle not of flesh and blood, but of the spirit. More real than anything we see in the natural. So do not enter this battle with a picnic basket. Do not think that you can fight the enemy alone. Heed the words of Scripture and put on God's full armor so that you are prepared for battle and can stand strong on the battlefield.

Paul envisions a Roman soldier suiting up for battle. The infantryman knows better than to saunter onto the battlefield wearing nothing but a robe and sandals. He takes care to prepare. Belt. Armor. Shield. Sword. He takes every weapon into the conflict. All are important. All are necessary. Take the belt but leave the helmet, and you lose your head. Take the sword but forget the shield, and you are vulnerable to an arrow. Take the shoes, but forget your sword? Well, you better just run. A soldier must suit up and be prepared.

So must we! Dare we saunter into the day with no protection? Dare we wander into enemy territory with no weapon? Not if we want to stand strong. Every battle, ultimately, is a spiritual battle. Our enemy is not passive or fair. He is active and deceptive. He has designs and strategies.

Consequently, we need a strategy as well. Second Corinthians 10:3–4 speaks of this spiritual battle we are in.

How are we not to fight? _____

_____

What is the purpose of our weapons? _____

_____

Who is our enemy? The one who turned on God, deceived Adam and Eve, and threatens our hearts today. The one who comes to steal, kill, and destroy. Satan.

But take heart. We have a promise that we can hold on to in the midst of the battle.

GOD'S PROMISE:

I have given you power over the enemy.

MY PROMISE:

I will acknowledge Satan but worship God.

One of my high school summers was spent as a roustabout in the West Texas oil field laying pipeline. A large ditch-digging machine would go in front, trenching a trough five feet deep. We would follow behind, shoveling out the excess dirt and rocks.

At some point the ditch-digger did more than break ground; it dislodged a rattlesnake's nest. Someone saw it and shouted, and you have never seen guys scramble out of a hole any faster. One of the workers launched his shovel like a javelin and beheaded the snake. We stood on the higher ground and watched as the snake—now headless—writhed and twisted in the soft dirt below.

Now, I know what you are thinking. "Thanks for the inspirational image, Max. Just what I needed to put some hope in my day."

Granted the picture is not inspirational, but it is hopeful. Those few moments in the West Texas summer are a parable of where we are in life.

Allow the snake to represent the devil. Not hard to do. John calls Satan *"that old snake who is the devil"* (Revelation 20:2).

Allow the spade of the shovel to represent the cross of Jesus. Paul gives us the good news. Only he does not say the snake is beheaded—but that the snake is disarmed.

According to Colossians 2:15, who did God disarm? _____

_____

How did He do this? _____

_____

What the worker did to the snake, our great God did to the devil. There was no slipping away into the shadows for him. There was no sending him away in the quiet. No, Jesus shamed the tormentor of our hearts publicly. One version even says, "He stripped all the spiritual tyrants in the universe of their sham authority at the Cross, marching them naked through the streets" (Colossians 2:15 MSG).

No matter how you translate the verse, the message is the same: the devil is a defeated foe.

The Bible traces Satan's activities to a moment of rebellion that occurred sometime between the creation of the universe and the appearance of the snake in the garden. Genesis 1:31 (NIV) says:

_____ **saw all that he had made, and it was** _____.

In the beginning, everything was good. Every drop of water, every tree, every animal, and, by extension, every angel. Yet, sometime between the events described in Genesis 1 and 3, an angel led a coup against God and was cast from heaven. The prophet Ezekiel describes the downfall:

> This is what the Sovereign LORD says: "You were the seal of perfection, full of wisdom and perfect in beauty. You were in Eden, the garden of God.... You were anointed as a guardian cherub, for so I ordained you. You were on the holy mount of God; you walked among the fiery stones. You were blameless in your ways from the day you were created till wickedness was found in you" (Ezekiel 28:12–15).

This being was in Eden, was anointed as a guardian angel, dwelt upon God's holy mountain, and was blameless from the day he was made until the day wickedness appeared. Who can this be but Satan? This prophecy is nothing less than a description of the fall of the devil. Lucifer's heart became proud. He was not content to worship; he had to be worshiped. He was not content to bow before God's throne; he had to sit upon it. No wonder the Bible says that pride is the sin God hates the most. No wonder Paul urged Timothy not to be too quick to promote a new convert "or he may become conceited and fall under the same judgment as the devil."

Satan succumbed to pride and, as a result, he was cast out of heaven.

But though he is cast out of heaven, he is not out of our lives. He is very much alive today and on the prowl. First Peter 5:8 (NIV) says:

Be _____ and of _____ mind. Your _____ prowls around like a roaring lion looking for someone to devour

The devil comes only to steal and kill and destroy. You have obtained happiness? Satan wants to steal it. Discovered joy? He'll try to kill it. Love your spouse? Satan would love nothing more than to destroy your marriage. He is the enemy of your destiny and longs to be the destroyer of your soul.

So put on God's full armor with the belt of truth tied around your waist and the protection of right living on your chest. On your feet wear the Good News of peace to help you stand strong. And also use the shield of faith with which you can stop all the burning arrows of the Evil One. Do not be caught off guard or asleep on watch.

Learn to recognize his stench. Since he comes to steal, kill, and destroy, wherever you see heists, death, and destruction, turn to God in prayer. His name means "divider," so wherever you see divorce, rejection and isolation, now you know the culprit. Go immediately to Scripture. Stand on the promises of God regarding Satan.

My friend Carter Conlon has ministered in New York City for over two decades. Yet he spent many of his early years on a farm. He recalls a barnyard scene that illustrates the status of Satan. In the barn lived a bunch of cats. The mother of the cats would corral a mouse in the field where she would taunt and tease it until the mouse was exhausted. She would then bring the rodent to the kittens to teach them how to catch and kill it. Carter remembers how the mouse would, upon seeing the kittens, rise up on its hind feet and prepare to fight. The rodent would bare his tiny yellow teeth and flare his little claws. He then attempted a snarl and hiss. His only hope was to convince the kittens that he was something other than what he was: a defeated, wimpy, outnumbered mouse. He would have already lost. The kittens did not even have to fight to win the victory.

Jesus has already defeated the rat of heaven as well. Be alert to the devil, but do not be intimidated by him. Do not be shaken. Your hope is in the God who already defeated him. You just have to stand your ground. Have no fear, Mighty Warrior; the Lord is on your side. Believe this powerful promise from God:

"The God who brings peace will soon defeat Satan and give you power over him" (Romans 16:20 NCV).

And make this promise of your own:

I will acknowledge Satan but worship God.

QUESTIONS FOR REFLECTION:

1. What is the biggest battle you are facing right now in your life?

_____

_____

_____

_____

_____

2. What promise from the Bible can you use as a sword to defeat your foe in this battle?

_____

_____

_____

_____

_____

3. What promise from the Bible can you lift as a shield against the lies of the enemy in this battle?

_____

_____

_____

_____

Praying the Promise:

Father, You are the God who brings peace.
This You have promised me.
I acknowledge there is an enemy seeking to destroy my soul,
but I hold to the promise that greater is He who is in me
than he who is in the world.
And I know You will bring me safely through every struggle
and into Your promised peace.
Amen.

Chapter Three:

Made in God's Image

Some of you will find this hard to believe, but there was a time many years ago in which airport security was all but nonexistent. A person could walk into the airport, down the concourse, show a ticket to the attendant, and board the flight. There was no electronic screening. No X-ray machines. No security team to examine your bag or wave a wand over your shirt. Boarding a plane was as easy as boarding a city bus.

On one such occasion, I boarded a late night flight from San Antonio to Denver. I walked through what I thought was the correct gate, handed my ticket to a weary gate agent, boarded the flight, and fell fast asleep. I was snoozing before the plane was fully boarded. I never heard the welcome from the pilot or the seat belt instructions from the flight attendant. Only as the plane was nosing down did I begin to wake up. The flight attendant told us to return our seats to the upright position, fasten our seat belts; we were about to land in *Houston*.

Houston? I needed to go to Denver! How did that happen? Apparently a bizarre combination of events had conspired to take me to the wrong city. The Denver and Houston gates were side by side. The gate agent was inattentive. There was no electronic device to confirm my destination. I fell fast asleep once on board.

I exited the plane, exasperated and confused. I hurried to the ticket agent and asked two urgent questions: How did I get here? And how do I get where I am supposed to be?

Do more fundamental questions exist? *How did we get here? How do we get where we are supposed to be?* If we live long enough on this earth, these are two questions that every person asks. No matter where we are born or the path our life takes. From prince to pauper, these are questions for which we all desire an answer.

None of us asked to be here. Not one of us can recall a moment in which we determined, "I will exist as a human being." By the time we knew we were humans, we had been conceived, formed, delivered, cleaned up, diapered, fed, burped, and disciplined. We were years into our existence before it dawned on us to ask, "How did I get here? How did I happen? Whose idea am I?"

Soon thereafter, we began to ask the second question: "How do I get where I am supposed to be?" This world often does not feel right. People kill each other. Cancer robs children of their health. Bad people get rich. Good people go hungry. Something is awry. Is this as good as it gets? Is there something more than what I see? I am stuck in Houston. I need to be in Denver.

Where do we find the answer to these shaking questions? These questions that gnaw at our days and keep us up in the night. Who am I? Where am I going?

Scripture addresses both in its opening chapter, with this promise in Genesis 1:26 (NIV):

Then God said: "Let us make mankind_____, in our likeness."

God made us for a high and holy purpose. We reflect the image of God. Out of all the creatures God made, we, and we alone, are said to be made in His likeness. Within you and me is the essence of God Himself. A holy seed, a divine spark. We are pregnant with His nature.

It is for this reason that we are made. God created us to testify to the greatness of Himself. You do not exist to promote you. I do not exist to promote me. We exist to promote God. We are made in His image.

GOD'S PROMISE:

You are made in My image.

MY PROMISE:

I will embrace my role as God's image bearer.

In the beginning, God created the beauty and complexity of the galaxies. He set the solar systems into orbit. Scattered the stars throughout the heavens. Created the land and the seas, the beasts of the field and the foul of the air. All the earth was His creation, and He called it good. But when He created mankind, He called it VERY good. When God created Adam and Eve, He made them to be more like Him than anything else He made. He never declared: "Let us make oceans in our image..." Or, "Birds in our likeness…" The heavens above reflect the glory of God, but they are not made in the image of God.

I can imagine the grand spectacle now… He placed one scoop of clay upon another until a form lay lifeless on the ground. All of the Garden's inhabitants paused to witness the event. Hawks hovered. Giraffes stretched. Trees bowed. Butterflies paused on petals and watched.

"You will love Me, nature," God said. "I made you that way. You will obey Me, universe. For you are destined to do so. You will reflect My glory, skies, for that is how you were created. But this one will be like Me. This one will be able to choose." And then He breathed His own life into man.

Each of us "takes after" God in many ways. There is no exception to this promise. The tribesman, the mountain man, the businessman. The lady of the court, the lady of the night, the lady down the street. Every man and woman, born or pre-born, rich or poor, urban or rural, is made in the image of God. Some suppress the image. Others enhance the image. But all were made in the image of God in order to reflect the greatness of God.

Adam and Eve walked with God in a beautiful type of Paradise, a life free from sin, guilt, and shame. They shared His joys, His creation, His creativity. They could have continued in that way, living in incomprehensible closeness with their Creator.

But instead, they listened to a lie. A lie that slithered into this beautiful world. In the Garden they had options: the tree of life—life with their Creator free from the pain of sin and death—or the tree of the knowledge of good and evil. A tree from which God had warned them not to eat. Adam and Eve had already savored "good." So to take from this tree was to now taste the bitter poison of sin and evil. But this protective warning was twisted into a lie by the enemy of our souls—"God does not want you to know good and evil, because He does not want you to be like Him." The very God who created man *in His image*.

Now, this may seem an easy fib to recognize, like the crumb-covered child who assures you that it was certainly not *he* who got into the cookie jar. But this ridiculous lie is much subtler and wider spread than you may think. It is a lie that still goes on today. It dismisses the idea that man and woman are creations of great value created in God's own image. And instead, diminishes them to the mere result of happenstance and chance. No wonder the question, "Where did I come from?" still lingers in the world today.

Humanity was deceived. The lie was believed. And sin entered the scene. The arrival of sin distorted this image, but it did not destroy it. Our moral purity has been tainted. Our intellect is polluted by foolish ideas. We have fallen prey to the elixir of self-promotion rather than God-promotion. The image of God is sometimes difficult to discern. But do not think for a moment that God has rescinded His promise or altered His plan. Just as He created Adam and Eve, He created us in His image to bear His likeness and reflect His glory.

The apostle Paul tells us what we were created for in Ephesians 1:11 (NIV):

In him we were also _____, having been predestined according to _____ of him who works out everything in conformity with the purpose of _____.

To the degree that you live to the glory of God, life makes sense. But to the degree you do not, life stinks. Think about it. If you live to promote you, then you are never satisfied because no one ever enjoys enough recognition. There is always someone who does not notice us. Your coworkers may recognize your effort, but your boss may not. Your close circle of friends may applaud your moral standards but social media may not. Your wife may praise your parenting efforts, but your son in a huff may not.

But, if you live for the glory of God, then you pillow your head every night with a feeling of success. "Ahh, what a great day. I loved people to the glory of God. I cared for my family to the glory of God. I prayed to the glory of God."

Ephesians 2:10 (NIV) says that:

We are God's _____, **created in Christ Jesus to do** _____, **which God** _____ **in advance for us to do.**

And according to the Bible, you are good and valuable because God made you in His image. Period. It is not based on your looks, intelligence level, net worth, or spiritual piety. He cherishes you because you bear a resemblance to Him. He delights in you. It even says that He sings over you.

Imagine that, God singing over you!

Would you let this truth find its way into your heart? See yourself as God sees you.

Loved.

His creation.

Made in His image.

Shove aside the lies and welcome this word from God. You are unique in all of creation! You are different from the animals, so do not act like one. Do not be consumed with appetites of food, sex, or entertainment. You were made for more! The essence of God is within you, so let it out!

Would you let this truth define the way you see other people? Every single person you see was created by God to bear His image. Every person deserves to be treated with dignity and respect. This means that all people, the mentally ill, the elderly, the pre-born, the impoverished ... every person deserves to be seen for what they are: image-bearers of God. That lady who stole your parking space ... God made her. That sibling that constantly tries to get under your skin ... God delighted in his creation. That coworker that is so hard to get along with ... yep, God made her too.

Can you imagine the impact this promise would have upon the society that embraced it? What civility it would engender! What kindness and patience it would foster! Racism cannot flourish when people believe their neighbor bears God's image. The fire of hostility has no fuel when people see the loving Creator in the eyes of creation. Will a husband belittle his wife? Not if he believes she bears the stamp of God. Will a boss neglect an employee? Not if she believes the employee bears a divine spark. Will society write off the indigent, the elderly or the poor? Not if they believe —truly believe—that every human being is God's idea. And He has no bad ideas.

You are made in God's image. You are valuable and of great worth. It does not matter how your life started, whether planned or unplanned. What you have been through, or what people have said about you.

After Adam and Eve chose to know sin, God found them hiding in the Garden ashamed. He asked a very important question: "Who told you that you were naked?" Shame had entered the world. And now I ask you today. Who told YOU, you should be ashamed? Ashamed of your past. Ashamed of your birth. Ashamed of your looks, upbringing, or social status. Who told you that you do not have a purpose? That you came from nothing and are going nowhere? Who told you, you are not going to amount to much? You do not have what it takes. Who told you? Because it was not God. It was not the One who created you in His image. It was not the One who named you. And the voice of your Creator is the only one that really matters. And He made a promise to you.

You and I were made by God to make Him known. This is God's plan and He will fulfill it! Put your hope in this promise: You are made in the image of God. Romans 8:29 (NIV) promises that:

For those _____ foreknew he also predestined to be conformed to the image _____, that he might be the firstborn among many brothers and sisters.

We have an unshakable hope in this promise. We are not lost. We are not drifting in a galaxy of meaninglessness. We are created, loved, and destined to reflect the image of God. What a beautiful promise.

Now let's make our own promise in return.

I will embrace my role as God's image bearer.

QUESTIONS FOR REFLECTION:

1. If we are truly made in the image of God, what does that tell you about God? What are some of His characteristics that show up in us?

_____

_____

_____

_____

2. Do you see your life differently knowing you are created in the image of the Creator?

_____

_____

_____

_____

3. Answer the two questions we saw at the beginning of this chapter: How did I get here? And how do I get where I am supposed to be?

_____

_____

_____

_____

CHAPTER FOUR:

YOU WILL NOT DROWN

Bertha Bourlard was a passenger on the second most famous boat ever built—the *Titanic*. She was a young French girl living in Paris when she made the acquaintance of Mrs. Walter Douglas, the wife of the founder of Quaker Oats. Mrs. Douglas invited Bertha to travel with the family to the US and serve as their maid. Bertha gladly accepted.

And so she was a passenger on the *Titanic* on that fateful night of April 14, 1912. She remembered and would later describe the beautiful cabin, the ornate furniture, the meals and dances and luxury. She called the *Titanic* a "floating palace." But then came the "thump" as she called it. She was asleep. She assumed it was a storm. Suddenly the light went out and the sailors came, shouting and handing out life jackets. She responded to the warning. Not everyone did. The cabin next to hers was occupied by passengers who refused to leave. They were certain that the ship would survive.

When given the chance to board the lifeboat, they refused. They made the wrong choice. But Bertha made it through the icy waters to safety because she listened to the voice of the sailors.

In the turbulent and unexpected storms of life, God, too, is offering us a safe passage. After the fall of Adam and Eve, there came a time when the world itself was a torrent of sin, chaos, and violence. Genesis 6:5–7 (NIV) puts it like this:

The LORD saw how great the _____ of the human race had become on the earth, and that every inclination of the thoughts of the human heart was only _____ all the time. The LORD regretted that he had made human beings on the earth, and his heart was deeply troubled. So the LORD said, "I will wipe from the face of the earth the human race I have created—and with them the animals, the birds and the creatures that move along the ground—for I regret that I have made them."

Sin is the word the Bible uses to describe our conscious decision to rebel against God's will.

Sin is an attitude toward God that leads to violent acts toward God's children and creation itself. In one of his Psalms, David wrote:

There is no one who _____. God looks down from heaven on all mankind to see if there are any who _____, any who _____. Everyone has turned away, all have become corrupt; there is no one who _____, not even one (Psalm 53:1–3 NIV).

A more somber soliloquy could hardly be written than in that passage from Genesis: "Every inclination of the thoughts of the human heart was only evil all the time." Sin had ravaged the human condition. It had spread like a contagion over the people. And they had turned their hearts from God. What began with Lucifer had continued through the ages.

- Satan turned from God.

- Eve turned from God.

- Adam turned from God.

- People in the days of Noah turned from God.

- I turned from God.

- You turned from God.

The Bible's assessment of sin is simply this: universal and fatal. Everyone sins, and apart from God's help, everyone dies from sin. Who can claim a life of purity and holiness? No one.

We have done what Adam and Eve did. They did it first, and we've done it since. They committed the original sin, and we have committed our personal sins. Even Paul confessed that he often desired to do what is good but did not carry it out (Romans 7:18).

A convicting question in the Bible is found in the book of Proverbs:

Who can say, "I have kept my heart_____; I am_____?" (Proverbs 20:9 NIV)

Sin not only contaminates every human being, it corrupts the being of every human. It is not just that we sin, it is that we cannot stop sinning. We do good, for sure, but we cannot stop doing bad. Do you consider that to be an overstatement? Hyperbole? If so, take the holiness test. Can you resolve yourself to be sinless for a week? A day? An hour? The next five minutes? Neither can I.

What does Ephesians 4:8 say about our condition apart from God?

_____

_____

Set against the totality of human sin is the absolute purity of our divine God. To the degree that we are sin-filled, God is righteous. He is not just the Holy One; He is the *Most* Holy One. The angels in God's throne ceaselessly declare: "Holy, holy, holy is the LORD Almighty; the whole earth is full of his glory" (Isaiah 6:3).

The dilemma is clear: God is holy and we are not. God is righteous and we are wrong. God is sinless and we are sin filled. When God sees our unbridled sin, it breaks His heart. So, where does that leave us?

Do you feel shipwrecked on the shores of life? Lost in waves of guilt and hopelessness?

GOD'S PROMISE:

I will keep you from drowning.

MY PROMISE:

I will respond to increasing evil with increasing faith.

In the vast, dark valley of sin and evil that had consumed the world, one tiny candle glowed. From the garbage dump, a singular daisy grew. If humanity was a massive mud pit, there was one man who stood to the side and refused to get muddy. His name was Noah.

When we think of rivers of difficulty, our minds return to Noah and the flood. When we think about God's promises, our minds turn to Noah and the flood. Indeed, we cannot discuss the promises of God without discussing God's promise to Noah.

Everything about the story of Noah is monumental.

Begin with the boat. As long as a football field, taller than a two-story house and wider than a half a dozen semi-trucks side by side. The boat was six times longer than it was wide, a ratio still used by shipbuilders today. In contained one door that presumably had to be closed from the outside and a singular skylight. Considering that no boat had ever been built, only one word describes this project. Monumental.

Then there were the animals. Children's books typically depict two of each species walking up a ramp. *Au contraire.* Actually there were more: one pair of each unclean animal and seven pairs of the clean animals. The rhino. The hippo. The mosquito. (If only it had been overlooked.) Elephants. Rodents.

Geese and giraffe. Noah was told to populate the boat with a sampling of animals. Not mentioned in the Scripture, but not to be forgotten by us, was the hay for the horses and the nuts for the squirrels and the bananas for the monkeys. The place was a zoo. This was a monumental assignment. Big boat. Big task. But the boat and task were monumental because the floodwaters would be.

God told Noah to expect forty days and forty nights of rain. What began as a pitter-patter resulted in a flood that swallowed all the high mountains, all the living creatures and, most significantly, all the sinful people. A people consumed by sin and violence. They had flooded the earth with rebellion. Now God would flood the earth with water. This was God's word to Noah.

Build the ark. Load the animals. Get in the boat. The flood is coming.

In Genesis 6, right in the very midst of a world drowning in sin and violence, God promised Noah a safe place, a certain deliverance. In a story of monumental craft, task, and flood, there is monumental promise. God takes care of His people. He said,:

"I will establish my _____ with you, and you will enter the ark—you and your sons and your wife and your sons' wives with you" (Genesis 6:18 NIV).

Then we read:

Noah did _____ just as God commanded him (Genesis 6:22 NIV).

People of the Promise do this. When given the option of choosing between an evil world and a good God, they trust the good God. When He says build an ark, they do. When He says, "You will enter the ark," they believe that they will.

Some of you are modern-day Noahs. Noahs in your workplace, Noahs in your neighborhood, Noahs in your family. Everyone else has turned away from God, and you are turning toward Him. He has seen you. He has taken note of your heart and resolve, and you, like Noah, have found favor in the eyes of the Lord. You may not have favor in the eyes of your boss, spouse, or teacher, but you have favor in the eyes of God.

The promise of God through the story of Noah is this: We will not drown. He has sent us a rescue vessel as well. In our case, we are saved, not by a boat, but by Jesus Christ. He is our Ark. We enter into Him. We trust Him. His gangplank is made of Calvary's cross. The skylight is formed from an empty tomb.

He seals it shut from the outside. He, and He alone, keeps us safe from the evil that floods about us. When we trust the promises of God, we enjoy the unspeakable benefit of His Son.

May we, like Noah, be obedient to God's commands. It took Noah decades to build the boat, but he obeyed. He was the only one who believed God's warning, yet he obeyed. He was ridiculed by others, yet he obeyed. No one had ever seen an ark or a rainstorm, yet Noah obeyed. The ark of salvation was available to anyone who would heed God's warning. Noah would have made room on the ark for any person who would have listened, but no one did. No one but Noah.

The Noah story is our story. The world is corrupt. The judgment is sure. But the salvation is certain. God has provided us a way of escape.

Romans 3:23–24 (NIV) says:

For all have sinned and fallen short of the glory of God, and all are justified freely by _____ through the _____ that came by Christ Jesus.

What a beautiful ending to a seemingly hopeless situation. We have salvation and redemption available to us through Christ, just as Noah was saved from the flood. We simply need to heed His voice and come aboard.

After the flood, God put a reminder in the sky for Noah, just like the nighttime stars that would one day be a reminder to Abraham of God's promise to him. (God seems to like to leave His notes in places they cannot be missed.)

From that day on, each time a rainbow crossed the sky, it would be a reminder to us of God's beautiful promise. So have hope in God's promise to you. **When you go through rivers of difficulty, you will not drown.**

Noah and his family were People of the Promise. As a result, they were saved. May the same be said about us. In response to God's promise, let this be ours.

I will respond to increasing evil with increasing faith.

QUESTIONS FOR REFLECTION:

1. What tends to keep you from drawing near to God? Shame? Fear? Disappointment?

_____

_____

_____

_____

2. Read Romans 8:31–39. According to Paul, what is it that can separate us from God?

_____

_____

_____

_____

3. Do you wholeheartedly believe you have been forgiven? How does the truth of God's forgiveness cause you to act differently?

_____

_____

_____

_____

Chapter Five

We Are Saved by Our Faith

Remember the good ol' days when credit cards were imprinted by hand? Some, maybe most, of you do not. If not, ask an old person like me. The clerk would take your plastic and place it in the imprint machine, and *rrack-rrack*, the numbers would be registered and the purchase would be made. I learned to operate such a device in a gasoline station on the corner of Broadway and Fourth when I was fourteen years old. For a dollar an hour I cleaned windshields, pumped gas, and checked the oil. Yes, Virginia, gas-station attendants did those things back then.

My favorite task, however, was imprinting credit cards. There is nothing like the surge of power you feel when you run the imprinter over the plastic. I would always steal a glance at the customer to watch him wince as I *rrack-rracked* his card.

- You buy gas, *rrack-rrack*.

- You charge some clothes, *rrack-rrack*.

- You pay for dinner, *rrack-rrack*.

If the noise did not get you, the statement at the end of the month would. Thirty days is ample time to rrack up enough purchases to rrack your budget. And a lifetime is enough to rrack up some major debt in heaven.

- You yell at your kids, *rrack-rrack*.

- You envy your neighbor's success, *rrack-rrack*.

- You break a promise, *rrack-rrack*.

- You lie, *rrack-rrack*.

- You lose control, *rrack-rrack*.

- You cheat, *rrack—rrack*.

Further and further in debt.

How do I pay this blasted thing off?

There it is. That's the question. How do I deal with the debt I owe to God, Deny it? Find worse sins in others? Claim lineage immunity? Try to pay it off? We do not know the cost of sin. We do not even know how much we owe.

Talk about depressing. A financial liability is one matter, but a spiritual one? Sin has a serious consequence.

Heaven is a perfect place for perfect people, and that leaves us in a perfect mess. According to heaven's debt bill, we owe more than we could ever repay. Every day brings more sin, more debt, and more questions like this one in Romans 7:24 (NIV):

Who will rescue me from this body that is _____?

The realization of our moral debt can devastate us. It sends some people into a frenzy of good works. Life becomes an unending quest to do enough, to be better, to accomplish more. We attend church, volunteer at every outreach, tend to the sick, go on pilgrimages, go on fasts. Yet, deep within is the gnawing fear, "What if, having done all, I have not done enough?"

Other people respond to the list, not with activity, but unbelief. They throw up their hands and walk away. No God would demand so much. He cannot be pleased. He cannot be satisfied. He must not exist.

Two extremes. The legalist and the atheist. The worker, desperate to impress God. The unbeliever, convinced that there is no God. Can you relate to either of the two? Do you know the weariness that comes from legalism? Do you know the loneliness that comes from atheism?

Then what do we do? I suggest that we consider one of the sweetest promises in all of Scripture: Romans 4:5 (NRSV):

_____ is reckoned as righteousness.

God is not looking for the right works or the perfect morality. He is looking for faith. And when He finds it, He credits that person with righteousness. Belief is enough.

What an incredibly freeing promise. No guilt. No shame. No sin.

What a gift that would be! Like winning the greatest lottery in the history of humanity, and you did not even pay for the ticket! Your debt paid. Your sins forgiven. Righteous not because of your work, but because of your faith in God. Now, that is something you could put your hope in.

GOD'S PROMISE:

I credit your faith as righteousness.

MY PROMISE:

I will rest in the assurance of salvation.

This promise was given to the best-known figure in the Old Testament. He appeared in the Bible as the man Abram. He was a grown man before we know anything about him, seventy-five years old before his biblical narrative began. Lineage? Power? Neither was mentioned.

Which may be the point.

Abram, who became Abraham, was not righteous. Not special. Not inherently godly. He tended to be restless and was known to stretch the truth. He was, at this point, childless. He had yet to father a son, much less a constellation of them. Yet, he came to be regarded as the great patriarch of the Hebrew Bible, the spiritual forefather of our world's 12 million Jews and 2 billion Christians. His lack of pedigree gives hope to any person who lacks one as well. God was not looking for a powerhouse. He was looking for a man He could bless, and through whom He would bless millions. Abraham was this person.

God told Abraham to leave his father's country and go to a land he would show him. He told Abraham that he would bless him and make him a great nation that all the people on earth would be blessed through Him. So Abraham went. (See Genesis 12:1–4.)

This word to Abraham is noteworthy because of what God offered and what God required. He offered everything and He required only this: faith. There were no tangible obligations on the part of the recipient. Unlike the covenant of the law handed down on Mt. Sinai, there were no commandments that Abraham needed to follow in order to receive the blessing. This was a one-way, insanely generous bequeathing of God.

All Abraham needed to do was believe God. No easy assignment. Abraham did not have what Moses and the children of Israel would have. By the time they are called to have faith, God had spoken through the fiery bush and the ten plagues. Moses saw the frogs, the flies, and the hail that fell like missiles. So, when God told him to follow in faith, he had a track record to consider. Not so with Abraham. He had no knowledge of supernatural history. He had not seen the miracles you and I have seen. He did not have the advantage of a written Bible. He did not know the stories of Peter's redemption, or Paul's conversion, or the empty tomb of Christ. They were mere dots on the distant horizon.

Abraham was simply told to believe. It is no wonder that he came to be known as the Father of the Faith. At the beginning, that is all he had.

God promised to give Canaan to Abraham. Really? Canaan already had inhabitants. The dwellers of the land did not have a "For Sale" sign in their yard. They weren't planning to leave. And what about his wife? She couldn't get pregnant. How could he become a great nation when Sarah's womb was barren? Two problems: an occupied Canaan and an empty crib. Yet, rather than raise an objection, Abraham raised his hands in worship.

People of the promise do this. They respond before they know the facts. Noah gathered gopher wood and got to work. Abraham gathered stones and began to worship. They did not need to know how the promise would be fulfilled in order to worship the God who gave it.

The fact that Abraham did not ask the questions initially, however, does not suggest that he did not ask them eventually. A drought caused him to move to Egypt where his faith was tested. And, quite honestly, he flunked the test. He lied about his wife to Pharaoh and when Pharaoh learned of his deceit, Abraham was banished back to Canaan. Even though his entourage grew, his faith struggled. Genesis 15:1–6 (NIV) puts it this way:

After this, the word of the LORD came to Abram in a vision: "Do not be _____, Abram. I am your shield, your very great reward." But Abram said, "Sovereign LORD, what can you give me since I remain _____" and the one who will inherit my estate is Eliezer of Damascus?" And Abram said, "You have given me no children; so a servant in my household will be my heir." Then the word of the LORD came to him: "This man will not be your heir, but _____ _____ will be your heir." He took him outside and said, "Look up at the sky and count the stars—if indeed you can count them." Then he said to him, "So shall your offspring be." Abram _____, and he credited it to him as righteousness.

Press the pause button on that scripture and think about the language. Abram's belief was credited to him as righteousness. To credit something is to make payment for it.

Abraham had, not a credit card debt, but a spiritual debt. He sinned. He was a good man, I am certain, but not good enough to go debt free.

Every time he cursed his camel. *Rrack-rrack*

Every time he flirted with a handmaiden. *Rrack-rrack*

Every time he wondered where in the world God was leading him and does God even know where in the world he is headed. *Rrack-rrack*

But for all the bad things Abram did, there was one good thing he chose to do. He **believed**. He put his faith in God. And because he believed, a wonderfully unspeakably great thing happened. He was credited with righteousness.

This has huge ramifications. If Abraham was made righteous, not because of works, but because of faith, what does that mean for us? In Romans 4, the apostle Paul tells us that we too have received that promise, because we are heirs of Abraham. He is the Father of us all. Therefore the promise of righteousness comes by faith, and is the guarantee of all those who have the faith of Abraham.

That means if God credits our faith, like Abraham's, as righteousness, then gone is the fear of falling short. Gone is the anxious quest for right behavior. Gone are the nagging questions: "Have I done enough? Am I good enough? Will I achieve enough?"

The God of Abraham is not a God of burdens, but a God of rest. He knows we are made of flesh. He knows we cannot achieve perfection. The God of the Bible is the One who says:

"**Come to me, all you who are weary and burdened, and I will _____. Take my yoke upon you and learn from me, for I am gentle and humble in heart, and you will _____ for your souls. For my yoke is _____ and my burden is _____**" (Matthew 11:28–30).

Don't your shoulders feel lighter just hearing that? You do not have to carry the heavy burden of your sins and shame. You are not able to. You are not meant to. But Jesus can, and He offers to do so. Just simply put your faith in Him.

When you lose your temper with your child, Christ intervenes. "I paid for that." When you tell a lie and all of heaven groans, your Savior speaks up, "My death covered that sin." As you lust over someone's center-fold, gloat over someone's pain, covet someone's success, or cuss someone's mistake, Jesus stands before the tribunal of heaven, points to the blood-streaked cross. "I have already made provision. I have paid that debt. I have taken away the sins of the world."

What a gift. And the only reciprocation for such a gift is living a life that is a result of a grateful heart. We are not as quick to go down the wrong path, not because we fear wrath, but because we realize the One who is asking us not to is the very One who paid the price of our sin. We are less likely to yell at our spouse when we remember that He who loved and forgave us is the One who asked us to love others. We live from the overflow of this revelation. We live from a heart of love for the One who paid our debt.

Our righteousness is not reliant upon a shaky foundation of human achievement. No, it stands on a firm foundation of faith in Christ. So, stand on this promise. Or, better said, take this promise to the bank. As you consider the insurmountable debt you owe, the debt you can never pay, let this promise sustain you: "Faith is reckoned as righteousness" (Romans 4:5 NRSV). And let this be our promise back to Him: "I will rest in the assurance of salvation."

QUESTIONS FOR REFLECTION:

1. What does it mean to believe God?

_____

_____

_____

_____

2. "Jesus died for my sins." Do you truly believe this? How do you show it?

_____

_____

_____

_____

3. Abraham believed a specific promise from God—that God would give him a son. What specific promise will you believe today?

_____

_____

_____

_____

_____

PRAYING THE PROMISE:

Father, I thank You for sending Jesus to make the way for my salvation.

My sins are no match for Your saving grace.

I am forgiven. My debts have been paid.

My destiny is secure because I have chosen to believe Your promise of eternal life

for all who place their hope in Jesus.

Thank You for helping me rest in the finished work of the cross

and the assurance of my salvation.

Amen.

Chapter Six:

Everything Works for the Best

Some time ago, I made a special visit to the American Hotel in Jerusalem. I was in Israel with a long list of places to visit and sights to see. But at the top of the list was a visit to the lobby of the American Hotel. I placed it on my itinerary not because I, too, am an American. Not because the food of the restaurant is tasty or the facility is particularly nice. The food is tasty and the establishment is terrific, but I went for another reason. I wanted to see the handwritten lyrics that hang on the wall, framed and visible for all to see.

———

Horatio Spafford wrote the lyrics, never imagining that they would become the words to one of the world's best-loved hymns. Then again, he likely never imagined that he would have to write an anthem to the providence of God. Spafford was a prosperous lawyer and Presbyterian Church elder. In 1871, he and his wife, Anna, suffered tragic losses in the Chicago fire. In November of 1873, Anna and their children set sail for Europe with a group of friends. Horatio stayed home to care for business. He would journey afterward to meet them. On November 21, he received a telegram from his wife that read: "Saved alone. What shall I do?" He soon learned that the ship had collided with a British vessel. The boat on which his family traveled sank. The four daughters drowned and only his wife survived. He left for England to bring Anna back home. En route, while sailing on the ship, he wrote the lyrics to a song that became an enduring hymn of hope.

He and Anna eventually moved to Jerusalem to form a Christian society designed to minister to the needs of all people. In time, the group expanded and moved into a large house outside the city walls. The house became a hostel, then a hotel. It still stands, and it still serves as the display location for these words written by a grief-stricken man on a storm-tossed sea.

When peace, like a river, attendeth my way,

When sorrows like sea billows roll;

Whatever my lot, Thou hast taught me to say

It is well, it is well, with my soul.

How can a man who has lost everything pen those beautiful words? How can you say with honesty, "It is well with my soul," in the midst of tragedy, pain, and the storms of *your* life?

Consider this. God is carrying the very cosmos toward a desired objective. We are not frozen or suspended in time. Nor are we orbiting about on a cyclical history. God is walking His plan down a defined purpose like a train engineer would move his train down a track.

As Paul says in Ephesians:

In him we were also _____, having been predestined according to the _____ of him who works out everything in conformity with the purpose of _____ (Ephesians 1:11–12 NIV).

The phrase "works out" comes from the Greek word *energeo*. God is the energy and energizing force behind everything. No moment, event, or detail falls outside of His supervision. He stands before the universe as a symphony conductor stands before the orchestra, calling forth the elements to play their part in the divine reprise.

God is the One who "causes His sun to rise on the _____,

and sends rain on the _____" (Matthew 5:45 NIV). God is the one who numbers the sparrows and feeds the birds (Matthew 6:26; 10:29). God is the One in charge of everything, even the details of your life.

So, if God is in charge, why do these storms come our way? How do we find hope in the midst of tragedy? Where do we find peace when we are plagued with questions that cannot be answered?

During times like these, we can anchor our soul to the promise found in the Old Testament promise:

"I'll see to it that everything works out for the best." (Isaiah 54:17 MSG)

God's Promise:

All things will work together for good.

My Promise:

I will trust God in difficult seasons.

Joseph was a man who walked through far more than his fair share of difficulty. His life story was a roller coaster of highs and stomach-dropping lows. Maybe you remember this story from the Old Testament.

Joseph had favor with his father and was given a brilliant coat of many colors as a gift.

A beautiful robe, a robe of honor and distinction. His brothers disliked his dreams, swagger, and obvious favor, and decided to throw him into a pit and sell him.

Joseph ended up on an Egyptian auction block and raffled like a farm animal. The great-grandson of Abraham was auctioned off to the highest bidder.

Even so, he landed on his feet. He worked his way to the top of Potiphar's household. But then the mistress of the house put the hanky-panky move on him. When he refused, she accused him of molesting her. Her husband took her side over Joseph's and tossed him in prison. Joseph landed in jail for a crime he did not commit.

Still, he landed on his feet. He became a model prisoner. He made his bed, made friends, and made a good impression on the warden who recognized him as Inmate of the Month and promoted Joseph to Convict-in-Charge. He had befriended two men from Pharaoh's court, a butler and a baker. Joseph asked the butler to put in a good word for him when he was released. The butler agreed. Joseph's heart raced, his hopes ran high. He kept an eye on the front door, expecting to be released any minute.

But Genesis 40:23 says:

The chief cupbearer, however, did not _____ Joseph; he _____ him (Genesis 40:23 NIV).

Joseph languished in prison for two years with no word, no hope, and no solution.

Two years! Plenty of time to give up. Plenty of time to give in to despair. Plenty of time to wonder: *Is this how God treats His children? Is this God's reward for good behavior? Do your best and this is what you get? A jail cell and a hard bed.*

If Joseph asked such questions, we do not know. But if you ask those questions, you are not alone. The soil of affliction gives rise to some thorny plants. "Does God know what I am passing through? If God knows, does He care?"

Have you asked it? You weren't thrown in jail, but you were placed in a hospital, went into bankruptcy, lost a job, lost a spouse, or, then again, maybe you were thrown in jail. And you wonder: "I believe in God. Is He aware? Does He care?"

In theological textbooks, these questions are discussed under the heading of *God's providence.*

What is God's ongoing relationship with His creation?

Does He preserve it? Manage it? Maintain it? Is He actively involved with and related to His creation on a daily basis?

Deism says "no." God created the universe and then abandoned it.

Pantheism says "no." Creation has no story or purpose unto itself; it is only a part of God.

Atheism says "no." Not surprisingly, the philosophy that dismisses the existence of a god will, in turn, dismiss the possibility of a divine plan.

Providence, on the other hand says, "Yes, there is a God. Yes, this God is personally and powerfully involved in His creation."

In Hebrews 1:3 (NIV), we read:

The Son is the radiance of _____ and the exact representation of _____, sustaining all things by his powerful word. After he had provided purification for _____, he sat down at the right hand of the Majesty in heaven.

The verb "sustains" means to carry or bring. It is to say that Jesus is directing it toward a desired aim. He is carrying it along. He exercises supremacy over all things. God is the One in charge of everything, even the details of our lives.

So, if God is in charge, why was Joseph in prison? Why does He permit challenges to come your way? Wouldn't an all-mighty God prevent them? Not if they are for His higher purpose. It was through suffering that Joseph came to be God's tool of rescue to the Hebrew people.

Remember the rest of the story? When Pharaoh was troubled by his dreams, the butler who met Joseph in prison finally recalled his promise to Joseph. He mentioned Joseph to the Pharaoh and, as fast as you can say providence, Joseph went from prison to palace. He interpreted the dream, which was a forecast of a famine.

Pharaoh was so amazed by Joseph that he pushed him straight to the top of the ladder, promoting him to prime minister. Joseph successfully navigated the famine crisis and saved not just the Egyptians, but his own family of Jacob. Years later Joseph would tell his brothers:

"You intended to harm me, but God intended it _____ to accomplish what is now being done, the _____ of many lives" (Genesis 50:20 NIV).

Two words at the heart of this verse reveal the promise of providence: "BUT GOD."

"You intended to harm me, **BUT GOD**..." What was intended as harm became good, why? Because Joseph kept God in the middle.

Can I urge you to do the same? I am sorry for the pain that life has given to you. I am sorry that your parents neglected you. I am sorry that the man abused you. I am sorry that someone said "I do" on your wedding day, but said "I do not" every day afterward. I am sorry you ended up in Egypt. But if the story of Joseph teaches us anything, it is this: We have a choice. We can wear our hurt or wear our hope. We can dress ourselves in our misfortune, or we can clothe ourselves in God's providence.

Centerpiece your testimony with a "but God." The company is downsizing, **but God** is still sovereign. The cancer is back, **but God** still occupies the throne. The finances are tight, **but God** is my provider. My parents did not want me, **but God** will never leave me. I was a jerk during the first years of my marriage, **but God** is showing me how to lead a family. I was an anxious, troubled soul, **but God** has been giving me courage.

The brothers had every intention to bring harm to Joseph. But God, in His providence, used their intended evil for ultimate good. He never robbed the brothers of their free will. He never imposed His nature upon them. But nor did He allow their sin and their sin nature to rule the day. He rerouted evil into good. God uses all things to bring about His purpose. He will not be deterred in His plan to sustain and carry creation to its intended glory.

The ultimate proof of providence is the death of Christ on the cross. Everyone thought the life of Jesus was over—**BUT GOD**. His Son was dead and buried, but God raised Him from the dead. God took the crucifixion of Friday and turned it into the celebration of Sunday. God can take you, too, from Friday to Sunday. From the pit to the palace. From broken to beautiful. From wrecked to redeemed.

Can He not do a reversal for you? Can He not use your dark places as part of His purpose? He certainly can. And He will. Trust in God's promise:

"I'll see to it that everything works out for the best" (Isaiah 54:17 MSG).

Everything means just that. Everything. Yes, even that difficult situation that's coming to your mind right now. He can take what you have experienced, and, in His love and power, turn it into something beautiful.

I pray whatever season you are walking through, that you would find what Joseph found—an unshakable hope in this unbreakable assurance.

Together, let's make this our own promise:

"I will trust God in difficult seasons."

And be assured...that which was intended to harm you, God will use for good.

QUESTIONS FOR REFLECTION:

1. When do you think Joseph began to see that God was in control of his life—before or after everything was set right?

_____

_____

_____

_____

2. Do you believe God can work out everything for good? If you do, how does that change the way you approach difficult situations?

_____

_____

_____

_____

_____

3. Name the biggest problem you are facing right now. Then complete this sentence: "But God

_____

_____

_____

_____

_____

PRAYING THE PROMISE:

God, just like You were with Joseph,
I know You are with me.
From pit to prison to palace,
You worked all things together for Joseph's good.
Lord, in the midst of my own trials and struggles,
remind me that Your eye never leaves me.
I place my trust in Your promise:
You will work out everything for my good.
Amen.

CHAPTER SEVEN:

THE PROMISE OF THE WRITTEN WORD

Have you ever made a bucket list? A list of things you want to accomplish during your lifetime? Visit the Grand Canyon…parasail off a mountain… eat an entire chocolate cake. We all have things in our heart we would like to do. Some big. Some little.

I am checking an item off my bucket list these days. I am taking flying lessons. I have a long way to go to learn how to be a pilot, but I am paying attention. After all, the motivation is very high. While the instructor hasn't entrusted the plane to me to fly, he has commissioned me to inspect it for pre-flight checkup. Now, this may not sound like that important of a job. But if the plane is not inspected right, a whole host of things could go wrong. And I do not know about you, but I would prefer to know that my plane is in tip-top condition when I am ten-thousand-plus feet in the air!

So before every flight, the pilot—or me, in this case—walks around the plane, searching for cracks, problems, loose nuts, or disengaged wings. There is a lot to remember. For that reason, I was happy to learn that the plane manufacturer provides a list. Were it not for the list, I would not know what to check for. Some things make sense like aircraft lights and engine oil. But magnetos? Avionics? Fuel selector valve? I needed to be told and I need to be reminded. I need the guidance.

I do not question the guidance. I do not look at the list and shrug, "They do not know what they are talking about." Or… "I think we can do without a fuel selector valve this time." I believe the maker of the plane knows more than I do, and I trust the manual.

Though we may not always take the time to read our manuals, we are given them so that we can more fully understand what we are doing. They provide answers to a number of questions, if we are willing to utilize them.

What does the mysterious light mean that just came on in my car? The manual lets me know whether I just need to check the oil or stop driving it and take it in to the shop. Why do I have a piece of wood left over from the bench I am building? The manual lets me know whether it is an extra replacement piece…or the very piece that keeps it standing. When we have a question, we trust that the maker has the answer in the manual.

Oh, that we would say the same about our Maker and His manual, the Bible. God has given us instructions, not a list in a cockpit, but a book called the Bible. He wrote His Word for us to read and obey.

The written word changed the way God used to relate to His people. Many of us are not privy to personal, divine conversations. Even though He still speaks through human lips, we cannot all have a preacher in our home, (my wife being the exception). But we can have a Bible. We can read God's decrees through the written word.

Can we believe this? Can we truly believe that the Bible is the Word of God? Many do not. Many say that the Bible is nothing but superstitions and stories. Others of us, however, have come to accept it as God's honest truth, and believe that God desires to and *will* direct us.

Second Timothy 3:16 (NIV) says:

All _____ is God-breathed.

What reasons do we have to truly believe this? The first is that Jesus believed it. We read in the book of Matthew that when the devil came to tempt Him, Jesus quoted Scripture. He said, "It is written...," He did not say, "It is said," or "I have heard..." He said, "It is written." Jesus had seen it for Himself recorded in Scripture, and spoke God's Word to combat the temptation of Satan.

Then when Jesus rose from the dead, He taught from Scripture. When He began to walk with two of the disciples after His resurrection, they did not realize it was Jesus at first. They were distraught about His death, so Jesus began to explain to them, through scriptures, everything that had happened.

In Luke 24:25–27 (NIV), Jesus said:

"How foolish you are, and how slow to _____ all that the prophets have spoken! Did not the Messiah have to suffer these things and then enter his glory?" And beginning with Moses and all the Prophets, he explained to them what was said in all the _____ concerning himself.

If Jesus considered Scripture to be reliable in fighting Satan and explaining God's plan, if He set upon it His own stamp of approval, what else is needed?

The second reason is that fulfilled prophecies confirm it. The Bible foretells of many things to come. These are called prophecies. God dares us to apply the test of prophecy to scriptures to prove if they are legitimate. Deuteronomy 18:21 says that you can prove if a prophecy is a true word from God by whether it comes to pass. It is as simple as that. If it does not come to pass, it was not from God, because everything He says will come to pass. If it does not, the prophet spoke presumptuously.

The Bible passes this test. Of the more than two thousand prophecies in the Bible, more than three hundred relate directly to the life of Jesus: His place of birth, His manner of death, His burial in the grave of a rich man. These and hundreds of others were fulfilled centuries after they were recorded.

Well-known mathematician David Williams, who studied the probability of the prophecies, once wrote, "The reason why prophecy is an indication of the divine authorship of the scriptures, and hence a testimony to the trustworthiness of the message of the scriptures, is because of the minúte probability of fulfillment."

The odds of three hundred prophecies being fulfilled in one person are staggering. Impossible really. Yet, records show that they came to pass through Jesus.

Third, changed lives affirm it. No book has impacted people like the Bible. From Augustine, who was a scoundrel, to John Newton, who was a slave-trader, to Abraham Lincoln, who was a simple farm boy, to Max Lucado, who was an ungrateful prodigal until he read about God's love for boys who have wandered from home and landed in a pigpen. The Bible changes lives.

But ultimately, you must make your own decision. See for yourself. Apply the principles of stewardship to your budget and see if you do not get out of debt. Apply the principles of fidelity to your marriage and see if you do not have a happier home. Apply the principles of forgiveness to your relationships and see if you are not more peaceful. Apply the principles of honesty at school and see if you do not succeed. Apply the Bible and see if you do not agree—the Bible works.

When our questions outnumber our answers, and our directional compass seems to be spinning, there is a solid promise we can stand on:

"I will _____ you and _____ you in _____ you should go" (Psalm 32:8 NIV).

GOD'S PROMISE:

I will guide your steps by My Word.

MY PROMISE:

I will read and heed God's Word.

The first day I get to heaven, there are a couple things on my checklist I would like to do:

- Worship Jesus.

- Hug my dad, mom, my brother, and sisters.

- Thank every person who prayed for me when I was a prodigal.

- Ask a few hard questions of the apostle Paul.

- Have a long conversation with Moses.

I would begin my Moses chat with this question, "What was the most dramatic moment of your earthly life?" I imagine he will give me the "You have got to be kidding" look, and ask me, "Just one?" "Yes, just one."

"Could I not give you the top three?" he would ask.

"No," I would insist, as if I could insist on anything from the man whose biblical byline reads: *Friend of God*.

I imagine he will sigh and smile and ask me to sit with him at the Pearly Gate Sidewalk Café. A crowd will gather at the sight of the woolly-haired man who still carries the same staff that once became a snake then became a staff again. He will stroke his beard and repeat my question so the onlookers can join our conversation.

"The most dramatic moment of my earthly life?" "Yes," I will affirm.

"Hmm," he will continue. "So many moments from which to choose. The burning bush that never burned up. The ten plagues, of which my favorite was the hopping frogs. Pharaoh saw them and nearly croaked." (I have a feeling Moses was pretty funny.)

He'll probably continue, "The day the Red Sea opened, then closed. The first feast of manna bread and quail burgers. Although I did grow weary of this diet after meal 6,402."

"Yes," I will say, "all fascinating moments. Your dull day was better than my best one. But of them all, which one was most dramatic?"

At that point he will look at me and, from beneath that grizzly salt-and-pepper beard, smile a wry smile. He will stand from his chair, hold the staff with one hand, and lift a finger into the air with the other. And, as if he was writing on an invisible tablet he will say, "The finger in the stone. That's it. The moment when God's finger carved the words into the stone."

Well, we'll have to wait to see the actual answer from Moses. But a strong case can be made for the Sinai moment. Up until that event, God had not spoken to His creation in that way. This was the first time God's instructions were put in writing.

Exodus 32:15–16 (NIV) says:

Moses turned and went down the mountain with the _____ of the covenant law in his hands. They were _____ on both sides, front and back. The tablets were the _____ of God; the writing was the _____ of God, engraved on the tablets.

I envision a lightning-like finger chiseling word after word into stone. Can you imagine seeing the hand of God writing a message to you? If Moses was able to move, it was only to gulp or pray. Upon completion, the stone tablets were given to Moses to, in turn, give them to the people. In doing so, God gave us this promise: He will guide us! Psalm 32:8 says, "I will instruct you and teach you in the way you should go."

These tablets containing God's words became guideposts to the children of Israel. God was giving them answers to a number of questions…questions about marriage, community respect, law and order, worship, and work. It was the first written guidance they had ever received. But it would not be the last. God was putting together a manual for us. A manual for life, filled with promises.

Many more records would be written. Many more prophesies made. Many of them written about Jesus, the One who would shed even more light on this ongoing narrative, and bring clarity to this unfolding Manual of Life. And it was written for us, you and me.

What a reassuring thing to hear! What hope this gives us! That God Himself would instruct us, teach us like a good father instructs a child, or a teacher imparts to a student. Guiding us along the path of life, offering us wisdom for life's journey. Caution and encouragement. Correction and praise. What an amazing thought, that we are not alone through the crazy twists and turns of life.

That's why I won't be surprised if the answer Moses gives me is "the finger in the stone." It changed everything. It gave us a compass for life. Jesus challenges us with these words:

"If you hold to _____, you are really my disciples. Then you will know the truth, and the truth will set you free" (John 8:31–32 NIV).

Freedom comes as we know the truth through God's Word. And isn't freedom a beautiful thing?

The word "freedom" itself lightens your shoulders, lifts your head, and puts a smile on your face. I may not be able to argue every theological and scientific question someone throws at me. There may be others who can do that. But I can tell you how my life was changed. I can give a walking, talking testimony that I once was lost but now I am found. I once lived in fear, but now I have peace. I once had a shadowy past, but now a bright future. I can tell you that I wouldn't trade this freedom for anything. Because when you have tasted freedom—like a prisoner who has seen the sunshine for the first time in a long time—there is just no going back. My life was changed when I met Jesus, when I was introduced to the living Word of God. The words on those pages have been a trustworthy compass in my life, ever leading me down the path of freedom.

They can be your compass too. God's promise is available to all who will receive His offer: "I will instruct you and teach you in the way you should go." (Psalm 32:8)

Together, let's make this our own promise in response.

I will read and heed God's Word.

Then let hope fill your heart as you trust Him to lead you.

QUESTIONS FOR REFLECTION:

1. How often do you read your Bible? How does reading God's Word shape your day?

_____

_____

_____

_____

2. Who do you turn to when you have questions about Scripture? Are you in regular conversations with others who study the Bible, so you can benefit from their questions and insights?

_____

_____

_____

_____

_____

3. What is your favorite Bible passage? Why does this mean so much to you?

_____

_____

_____

_____

_____

PRAYING THE PROMISE:

Father, through Your spoken word
all of the stars and planets and moons came into being.
Through Your written Word, the scriptures, You taught us how to live.
And through Jesus, You revealed to us the word made flesh,
the fulfillment of every promise.
Your Word is alive and active and sharper than a two-edged sword.
Your Word is a lamp unto my feet and a light unto my path.
Help me to understand and apply Your word to my life daily.
Amen.

CHAPTER EIGHT:

I AM AN HEIR OF CHRIST

The sixty-year-old body of Timothy Henry Gray was found under a Wyoming overpass two days after Christmas in 2012. There was no sign of foul play. No indication of crime or mischief. Gray was a victim of bad breaks and bad luck, a homeless cowboy who had died of hypothermia.

Except for this detail. He stood to inherit 30 million dollars. Gray's great-grandfather was a wealthy copper miner, railroad builder, and the founder of a small Nevada town you might have heard of: Las Vegas. His fortune was passed down to his daughter Huguette. She died in 2011 at the age of 104.

She left her $300,000,000 fortune to extended family members. At the time of Gray's death, the execution of the will was tied up in court. As things turned out, the man found dead under the railroad overpass was not poor after all. He may have been worth millions.

How does the heir to a fortune die like a pauper? Surely Timothy Gray knew his family history.

Was he in touch with his great aunt? Did it ever occur to him to investigate? You would. I would. Why, we might camp out at the doorstep of our dear distant relative. We would turn over every stone and read every document. We would make it our aim to access our inheritance, wouldn't we?

But do we?

Let's talk about your inheritance. For an inheritance to come to you, you have to accept it. It makes logical sense. But too many people are not receiving what has been given to them. Maybe you have been given an inheritance in the past. It is such a precious gift to know that someone who lived their life ahead of you wanted to leave you something. Regardless of whether it was a large gift or simply a small remembrance of your relationship, the natural response was to receive and cherish that gift.

Or maybe you were supposed to receive an inheritance, but for whatever reason, that inheritance was stolen from you. You never received the inheritance that was meant to be yours. Or could it be possible that you do not have a family inheritance waiting for you at all, because you do not have anyone around who would even think to leave you an inheritance?

No family name.

No family inheritance.

An heir to no one.

Well, let me be the bearer of good news: you have been given an incredible inheritance.

Regardless of the status of your natural inheritance, if you are Christ's, you are in God's family. If you are in God's family, you are an heir to God's fortune. You have a family name, and you have a family inheritance.

The apostle Paul said in Ephesians 1:13–14 (NIV):

You also were included in Christ when you _____,

the gospel of your salvation. When you _____, you were marked in him with a seal, the promised _____, who is a deposit guaranteeing our inheritance.

You are not a slave of God, though even that position would have marvelous benefits. You are not simply a servant of God, though the role would be sufficient. You are not simply a saint of God, though the title itself implies astounding grace. No, you are *sons and daughters* of God. You sleep in His house, eat at His table, and carry His name. You have a legal right to the family business and fortune of God. If you belong to Christ, then according to the Bible, you are Abraham's seed, and an heir according to the promise. You are no longer a slave, but God's child. And since you are His child, God has made you also an heir.

Look at Galatians 3:29 and 4:7. What promises are found in these verses?

3:29 _____

4:7 _____

Is that not great news? You have been adopted into the family. Because of God's love for you, when Jesus died on the cross, the will was executed and you were made a benefactor. You have a seat at the table of inheritance. So, what is this inheritance? In another passage, Paul reveals its value.

In Romans 8:16–17 (NIV) he writes:

The Spirit himself testifies with our spirit that we are _____. Now if we are children, then we are heirs— heirs of God and _____, if indeed we share in his _____ in order that we may also share in his glory.

You share in his inheritance. Everything He has, you have. What is the fortune of God? If there were to be an execution of His will, what words would the lawyer read?

- "Unending life," for starters

- "Boundless joy" would make the list

- "Perfect peace"

- "Unsearchable wisdom"

- "Contentment"

- "Love"

Every virtue we see in Jesus, we see in our inheritance. His love level is your love level. His joy supply is your joy supply. Need some peace? You and Jesus share the same peace reservoir.

Low on patience? Check your inheritance. You and Jesus have the same amount.

Now, if upon reading your inheritance you find yourself thinking, *That does not describe me,* then perhaps Timothy Gray is not the only one to miss out on an inheritance.

GOD'S PROMISE:

You are heirs of God and co-heirs with Christ.

MY PROMISE:

I will live out of my inheritance, not my circumstance.

God did some amazing miracles to free the children of Israel out of slavery. Then He took them through the wilderness, leading them to the edge of the Promised Land, and made this offer:

The LORD said to Moses, "Send some men to explore the land of Canaan, which I am _____ to the Israelites. From each ancestral tribe send one of its leaders" (Numbers 13:1–2 NIV).

God did not tell the Israelites to conquer, take, invade, subject, or secure the land. He was giving it to them. All they had to do was trust His promise and receive the gift. But they did not. It was a bad decision with a forty-year probation penalty. God left them to wander in the wilderness for a generation until a new breed of followers surfaced. Joshua was the leader of that generation. Upon the death of Moses, God reissued the Promised Land offer.

The LORD said to Joshua son of Nun, Moses' aide: "Moses my servant is dead. Now then, you and all these people, _____ the Jordan River into the land I am _____ to them—to the Israelites. I will _____ where you set your foot, as I promised Moses" (Joshua 1:1–3).

We typically think of Joshua as a mighty warrior "taking the land." It is more precise to think of Joshua "taking God at His Word." He took the land, for sure. But he did so because he trusted God's promise. The great accomplishment of the Hebrew people was this: they trusted their inheritance.

Is that to say they had no challenges? The Book of Joshua begs to differ. They had adversity and adversaries on every front. The Jordan River was wide. The Jericho walls were high. The evil inhabitants of Canaan were not giving up without a fight. Still, Joshua crossed the Jordan, brought down the walls of Jericho, and defeated the thirty enemy kings. He believed that God had given him the land. Every time he faced a challenge, he did so with faith, because he trusted his inheritance.

Even when God told them to walk around the wall of a fortified city for seven days (not attack the wall, not climb the wall—just walk *around* the wall), Joshua still trusted the promises of God. He knew God would keep His word, and that their inheritance hadn't changed just because a wall was in their way. They did not let it stop them. They kept their eyes on the promise of their inheritance.

What if you and I did the same?

If we are co-heirs with Christ, why do we struggle through life? Our inheritance is perfect peace, yet we feel like a perfect mess. We have access to the level of joy of Jesus, yet we plod along like cranky donkeys. God promises to meet every need, yet we still let giant walls of worry and fret cause us to run and cower in defeat. Why? I can think of a couple of reasons.

First, we do not know about our inheritance. No one ever told us about "the exceeding greatness of His power toward us who believe" in Ephesians 1:19. No one ever told us that we fight from victory, not for victory. No one told us that the land is already conquered. Some Christians never live out of their inheritance because they did not know they had one.

But now you do. Now you know that you were made for more than the wilderness. God saved you from Egypt, so that He could bless you in the Promised Land. Moses had to remind the people that:

"[God] brought us out of there in order to _____
[to Canaan]" (Deuteronomy 6:23 NIV).

There is a reason for our redemption, too. God brought us out so He could lead us in. He set us free so He could raise us up.

Joshua was given a gift: the land of milk and honey. He did not earn it or deserve it, but he was called to inhabit and indwell it. You have been given a gift: a relationship with the living God. You did not earn it, you do not deserve it…but God has called you to embrace and develop it. Joshua's decision is your decision. Will I inherit the land? Will I develop the gift? *Will I—with God's help—exploit God's territory?*

The land is yours. Take it. God's gifts are only ours when we accept them. Salvation is no treasure to one who won't receive it. And the Promised Land meant nothing to Joshua if he wouldn't enter it. He did not have to. Remaining in the wilderness was an option. The children of Israel turned away from the territory forty years earlier, they could turn away again. But instead, they chose to move forward.

To Timothy Gray, the man who famously forfeited his $300,000,000 inheritance, we would have said: "Hey, Mr. Gray, you are the descendant of wealth, the heir to a fortune. Get out from under this bridge and make your request. "

To us, the angels want to say: "Hey, Lucado! Yeah, you with the rotten attitude. You are the heir to the joy of Christ. Why not ask Jesus for help?"

"And you, Mr. Heavy-hearted. Are not you an heir to God's fortune of faith? Ask for some help, why don't you?"

"Mrs. Worrywart. Why do you let your fears steal your sleep? Jesus has abundant peace. Are you not a beneficiary of God's trust fund?"

You do not have to sleep under the overpass anymore. And you do not have to walk around that wall forever. You are a new person. Live like one. It is time for you to leave the wilderness. It is time for you to live out of your inheritance. The gift has been given. Will you trust it?

Ahh, therein lies the second explanation for our weaknesses.

Some of us do not believe in our inheritance. This was the problem of Joshua's ancestors. They really did not believe that God could give them the land. God told Joshua:

"Every place that the sole of your foot shall tread upon, _____, as I said unto Moses" (Joshua 1:2 KJV).

The implied reminder? *I made this offer to the people of Moses' day, but they did not take it. They chose the wilderness. Do not make the same mistake.*

Joshua did not. Much to his credit, he took God at His word and set about the task of inheriting the land. Do the same. Receive yours. You are embedded with the presence and promises of God. Do not measure your life by your ability, measure it by God's. Even though you cannot forgive, God can. And since He can, you can. You cannot break the habit, but God can. Since He can, you can. You cannot control your tongue, temper, or sinful urges, but God can. And since you have access to every blessing of heaven, you, in time, will find strength. Inherit your inheritance.

The wilderness mentality says, "I am weak and I will always be weak." People of the Promise say, "I was weak, but I am getting stronger." Wilderness people say, "I am a victim of my environment." Promised Land people say, "I am a victor in spite of my surroundings." Wilderness people say, "No one in my family succeeded; I guess I won't either." God's people say, "I am born into the victorious family of God." It is time for a generation of Christians to vacate the wilderness.

"[We] are heirs—heirs of God and co-heirs with Christ." So, together you and I can make this our own promise:

I will live out of my inheritance, not my circumstance.

QUESTIONS FOR REFLECTION:

1. Name three great needs you have in your life right now. Think of spiritual, physical, family, and financial needs.

_____

_____

_____

2. What does God have that could meet these needs? If you have a problem, God has a promise. What scriptural promise does God make about your situation?

_____

_____

_____

3. How does your perspective change when you live out of your inheritance instead of your circumstances?

_____

_____

_____

_____

CHAPTER NINE:

THE LORD IS WITH YOU

Do you ever feel small? Like a daunting task is looming large before you and you just do not feel adequately equipped for the job? Perhaps it is a task that calls for the work of a mighty champion, but you feel more like a wimp than a warrior.

Most of us can relate. I know I can. Somewhere I have a picture of the Mighty Mustangs freshmen basketball team. Not the varsity or junior varsity team, but the ninth grade team. In the same frame, you'll find two photographs, one of the first string and one of the second team. I was on the second team. Almost.

The B-team had ten uniforms and twelve players. Hence, two of us did not get to suit up for the B-team freshman games. The other no-uniform kid had thick glasses and a rotund girth. At least he had an excuse. I had decent eyesight and height, but the coordination of a rhinoceros. So in the team picture, I appear wearing cuffed Levi's and Hushpuppies.

I did not want to go to the photo shoot. Capture on film my place at the bottom of the pecking order? No thanks. But, just like I did not know how to pick-and-roll on the court, I did not know how to sneak out of the gym. The photographer positioned the team beneath the basket and asked the chubby kid and me to stand on either flank. *Click.* My place as a basketball nobody was documented for the ages.

But here is an important truth we often miss. God chooses to work with people who might look like "nobodies" in order to reveal just how big of a "somebody" He is. We often feel that we are just not enough. And we are not alone in that thinking. But more importantly, we are not alone, period. You see, God is with us. Throughout Scripture, He promises to be with us. What God said to Jacob He says to you:

"I am _____ and will _____ wherever you go" (Genesis 28:15 NIV).

What God said to Joshua, He says to you:

"As I was with Moses, so I _____; I will _____ leave you nor forsake you" (Joshua 1:5 NIV).

What God said to the nation of Israel, He says to you:

"Do not fear, for _____; do not be _____ for I am your God. I will strengthen you and help you; I will uphold you with my righteous right hand.... When you pass through the waters,_____" (Isaiah 41:10; 43:2 NIV).

One of the biggest lies of the devil is that God only uses special people. And like all lies of the devil, this one is based on a half-truth. God does use special people. The reason they are special is because God uses them. Listen to the Word of God:

You are _____. You are a royal priest, a holy nation, God's _____. As a result, you can show others the goodness of God, for he called you out of _____ into his wonderful light (1 Peter 2:9 NLT).

Do you understand how special you are? God loved us so much that even though we were dead because of our sins, He gave us life when He raised Christ from the dead. It is only by God's grace that you have been saved! And you cannot take credit for this; it is a gift from God.

Special has nothing to do with how you look, or what you can do, or how smart you are.

Special has everything to do with the fact that none other than the Master of the universe created you as a unique individual. The same God who drew rainbows across the rain-washed skies, who paints the morning sunrise and the evening sunset, the same God who scooped out the Grand Canyon with His fingers, who molded the Rocky Mountains with His hands and threw the Milky Way into the midnight sky, that same God created you.

And that same God is right beside you. And that means that you are somebody. And that you are fully equipped to take on the tasks before you. We do not base our beliefs on how we feel. We build them on the promises of God. They are unshakable.

This great and precious promise is found in the words of the angel to Gideon in Judges 6:12. He tells Gideon, "The Lord is with you." Let that sink in for a moment. You are never alone. And with God at your side, you have more than enough to face your battles and win your wars in whatever form they present themselves to you.

GOD'S PROMISE:

I am with you.

> ## My Promise:
>
> *I will lay claim to the nearness of God.*

Do you know how it feels to have the odds unfairly stacked against you? Sometimes the difficult feels impossible. I know that feeling. But I also know that, crazy as it sounds, sometimes when circumstances appear to be conspiring against us, it is actually just the hand of God preparing to prove His faithfulness. The Lord is mighty and powerful, and He delights in showing up big when things seem beyond hope. Think I am making this stuff up? Just look to the experiences of Gideon.

The odds weren't very good to start with, and then they got worse. Or better, depending on whose side you were on. Gideon was a simple farmer, albeit a happy one. He displayed no political ambitions, demonstrated no military interests, and yet God turned this farmer into a leader and used him to protect Israel.

Ever lurking nearby was a gaggle of rascals known as the Midianites, nomads who stole crops and herds from the Israelites and destroyed what they couldn't take with them. After years of being bullied, the Israelites cried out to God to deliver them, and God responded by calling Gideon. An angel sent from God found Gideon threshing wheat in a wine press. That's odd. Farmers threshed wheat in the field where the chaff could be blown away by the wind. Why would Gideon work in the wine press? Because he was afraid. He wanted to hide from the enemy. It is no wonder that the angel prefaced his remarks with this wonderful reminder:

"The Lord is with you, _____" (Judges 6:12 NIV).

Could you use that reminder? You are not hiding in a wine press, but you may be dreading the call from the doctor or wondering how you are going to pay the mortgage. You do not fear the enemy tribes, but you do fear the final exams or the grumpy supervisor. Do you feel all alone? You are not. You never have been and you never will be. Promises of God's presence are to Scripture what diamonds are to Tiffany's. They sparkle on every page.

Gideon needed a 20-carat version, so he said, "Pardon me, my lord, but how can I save Israel? My clan is the weakest in Manasseh, and I am the least in my family." He claimed to be a wimp from a family of wimps. He needed to be convinced that God was with him so he laid out this proposal. He said:

"Look, I will place a wool fleece on the threshing floor. If there is dew only on the fleece and all the ground is dry, then I will know that you will save Israel by my hand, _____" (Judges 6:37 NIV).

The next morning the ground was as dry as a bone but the fleece was sopping wet. Still not wanting to rush into this thing, Gideon prayed again. "Hey Lord, I do not want to get annoying, but let's try it the other way. I will leave the fleece out again tonight and in the morning if the ground is wet and the fleece is dry then I will know that I need to listen to you." The next morning the ground was covered in dew and the fleece was completely dry. And so Gideon began to think, "Wow, God must be serious here."

This is where the story gets really interesting. Gideon looked out over on his army of thirty-two thousand men and thought, "We can do this." And God said, "Not so fast Gideon. You have got too many men." (Too many men? How can you have too many men?) He told Gideon to announce:

"Anyone who _____ may turn back and leave Mount Gilead." So twenty-two thousand men left, while ten thousand remained (Judges 7:3 NIV).

Two-thirds of his guys packed their bags. Gone. Poof. They scatted faster than scalded cats. Gideon was down to ten thousand men. God said, "Still too many." He told Gideon to send the men to the river for a drink: those who knelt and lapped up the water like a dog were to go into one group and those who cupped the water and drank from their hands were to go to another group. Only three hundred of the soldiers drank from their cupped hands. Gideon was thinking, *Oh boy, I hope I get those who look like puppies when they drink*. Alas, it was not to be. God told Gideon to keep the men who drank from cupped hands and to send the rest home. In a matter of moments, his resources dropped by 95 percent!

Can you relate? I received an email this week from a dear friend, a dear unemployed friend.

After more than a decade in his field, he lost his job and is beginning to lose his hope. In the last three months he has been turned down five times. Matters seem to be getting worse, not better.

And you?

Are your bills increasing, not decreasing? Is your arthritis worsening, not improving? Is the criticism you receive growing, not diminishing?

If so, then Gideon is your new hero. He was left with three hundred men. The only thing they had going for them was that they drank politely. His resume was weak. His army was small. But Gideon's God was great.

God told Gideon to sneak into the enemy camp for a reconnaissance mission. Gideon took one of his leaders and eavesdropped on a campfire conversation. He overheard one soldier say to another, "I had the strangest dream last night. I dreamt that a loaf of barley bread rolled down the hill into the camp and flattened one of our tents." The second guy said, "Your dream can only mean one thing, Gideon and his men are going to whoop us." (See Judges 7:12–15.)

Gideon took the dream as a sign from God and went back to the camp to rally the troops.

According to Judges 7:15 (NIV):

**When Gideon heard the dream and its interpretation, he _____
_____. He returned to the camp of Israel and called
out, "Get up! The LORD has given the Midianite camp into your hands."**

He divided his three hundred men into three groups, a hundred in each. He gave each man a horn and a clay jar with a torch in it. Just after midnight they surrounded the Midianite camp and, on the given signal, they blew their horns and broke the clay jars, revealing the torches. The Midianites panicked, the Israelites blew their horns again, and the Lord caused the warriors in the camp to start fighting each other. Those who weren't killed fled in confusion.

Do not you love it when a plan comes together? Gideon learned what God wants us to learn. He is enough. We do not need a large army. We do not need abundant resources. All we need is the presence of God. His presence tilts the scales in our favor. Guard against thinking that God is far away, removed from us. Indeed, He indwells the farthest galaxy, but He also inhabits the space next to you as you ponder these words. He is simply everywhere all the time. Which means, He is with you as you face your armies. With you as you are wheeled into surgery. With you as you enter the cemetery.

Psalm 23:4 (NIV) says:

**Even though I walk through _____, I will fear no
evil, for _____, your rod and your staff, they
comfort me.**

We may not understand God's ways and, like Gideon, we have our questions. But let's remember that one person plus God is a majority. God's odds are the best. And God is with you. Always. So hold on to this precious promise:

"The Lord is with you."

And in so doing, make your own promise:

"I will lay claim to the nearness of God."

QUESTIONS FOR REFLECTION:

1. Look at 2 Corinthians 12:9. When does Paul say God's strength is seen the most?

_____

_____

_____

2. What are your greatest weaknesses? How does the nearness of God make you strong in these areas?

_____

_____

_____

_____

3. What is the biggest battle you are facing right now? Are you willing to become weak so that God can be strong for you?

_____

_____

_____

_____

Praying the Promise:

Jesus, Your grace is sufficient for me no matter what I face.
When I am weak, You are strong.
When I feel less than, You are more than enough.
Your power is at work in my life, transforming me into Your likeness.
Help me to surrender my weaknesses to You each and every day.
Amen.

CHAPTER TEN:

THE LORD REDEEMS ME

My big brother used to pick on me. No day was complete unless he had made mine miserable. He would trip me as I entered the room. He would yank back the covers on my just-made bed. He would wrestle me to the floor and sit on my chest until I couldn't breathe. When his bike tire was flat, he would steal my bike. He would kick me beneath the dinner table and when I kicked back, I got caught while he feigned innocence. Thanks to him I learned the meaning of the word "wedgy." His first waking thought was: "How can I pick on Max?" He stole my allowance. He called me "sissy." He threw grass burrs at me.

But all of his cruel antics were offset by one great act of grace. He picked me to play on his baseball team. Everyone else that day on the field was in middle school; I was a third grader. Everyone else could handle a baseball bat. I never got a hit. Everyone else could pitch, catch, and steal bases. I was slow, clumsy, and most of all, I was a little kid. On the pecking order of the baseball diamond I dangled from the lowest rung.

So, when it came time to pick teams, I braced for the worst. The selection of summer baseball teams is enough to scar the psyche of a kid. It works like this. Two players, presumably the best players, begin calling out names. "I get Johnny." "I get Tommy." "I want Jason." "I will take Eric."

Johnny, Tommy, Jason, and Eric strut and swagger in the direction of their respective captains and strike the cool-kid pose. They deserve to. They were chosen first.

The winnowing process continues until, one by one, the last kid is standing. That day, that kid, I just knew, would have freckles, red hair, and be called Max. Especially since my brother was one of the captains.

But a miracle happened. When angels discuss mighty acts of divine intervention, this moment makes the list. Along with the stories of the Red Sea opening and Jesus walking on water is the moment that my brother chose me. Not first. But far from last. He still had plenty of good players to pick from.

But for a reason known only to him and God above, he chose me. I went from the back of the pack to the front of the line, all because he called my name.

He did not pick me because I was good. He did not select me for my skill or baseball savvy. He called my name for one reason and one reason only. He was my big brother. And on that day he decided to be a good big brother.

You might say he chose to be my "kinsman-redeemer." Then again, you would never say that.

You have likely never heard that phrase, much less used it. Yet, you would be wise to make it a part of your glossary. God's list of promises to you includes this one: He will be your kinsman-redeemer. But first you must ask your kinsman-redeemer to take you into His care. He has promised to do so.

Psalm 34:22 (NLT) says:

The Lord will _____ those who serve him.

But what does it mean to serve Him? Is the Psalmist saying that we will be redeemed if we first prove ourselves worthy to be treated as part of the family of God? Does being a son or daughter of the Most High require a certain social or economic status? A proven track record? A supernatural skill set?

Or could it be that none of those traits are what is required because they are all outward expressions, and God is more interested in matters of the heart?

If you are worried that you are not worthy of God's love, I have got news for you—you are right. He does not need you on His team. He does not need me, either. Let's face it, none of us are the top prospects of our class. We are not the top picks of the first round of the draft. We all come with plenty of weaknesses in our game. If our stats were being tracked, we would have plenty of errors, strikeouts, and blown saves in the books.

But you know what is so remarkable about God? He does not care about any of that, because it is not about what you can do for Him. It is about what He can do for you, and through you, when you surrender your heart and give Him control.

A willing heart. A humble stance. An invitation for Him to come in and be with us. These are the things He seeks when evaluating the players around Him. You might say that Jesus is the perfect big brother. When He spots you on the field, He makes certain you are on the team. His team. The winning team!

I never asked my brother what motivated him that day on the baseball diamond. I would like to think that he picked me because of my talent. But he did not. He picked me because that's what a good big brother does.

Maybe he took a cue from Jesus. Maybe we can each do the same today as we live out our faith knowing we have a kinsman-redeemer looking out for us.

So if you are feeling a bit shaky like you are just not good enough to make God's team, take heart. We do not need to live our lives based on our feelings. We choose to live them on the unshakable promises of God.

GOD'S PROMISE:

The Lord will redeem those who serve Him.

MY PROMISE:

I will turn to Christ, my kinsman-redeemer.

You know that saying, "It is not what you know, but who you know that matters"? It is remarkably true today. And it was true for Ruth and Naomi, two women who seemed to be running out of luck, but instead were about to run into the provisions of God.

Here is the scene:

Two figures crested the horizon of the Judean desert. One an old widow, the other a young widow. Road dust powdered their cheeks. The two huddled together, for all they had was each other.

Ten years prior, a famine had driven Naomi and her husband out of Bethlehem. They sold their land and migrated to the enemy territory of Moab, where the couple found fertile soil to farm and girls for each of their two sons to marry. But tragedy struck. Naomi's husband died. So did her sons.

Naomi resolved to return to her hometown of Bethlehem. Ruth, her daughter-in-law, determined to go with her.

The pair could hardly appear more pitiful as they entered the village. No money. No possessions. No children to care for them. No farm to cultivate. In the twelfth century BC, a woman's security was found in her husband and her future secured by her sons. These two widows had neither. They'd be lucky to find a bed at the Salvation Army.

But then a bachelor entered the story: Boaz. He was educated and wealthy, and ran a profitable farm with a sprawling house that was fully paid for. He was living the life.

But then he saw Ruth. She was not the first immigrant to scavenge grain from his fields. But she was the first to steal his heart. Her glance caught his for just a moment. But a moment was all it took. Eyes the shape of almonds and hair the color of chocolate. Face just foreign enough to enchant, blush just bashful enough to intrigue. His heart pounded like a kettle drum solo and knees wobbled like jelly. As fast as you can turn a page in the Bible, Boaz learned her name, story, and Facebook status. He upgraded her workstation, invited her for supper, and told the foreman to send her home happy. In a word, he gave her grace. At least that is the word Ruth chose when she said, "Oh sir, such grace, such kindness—I don't deserve it. You have touched my heart, treated me like one of your own. And I do not even belong here!" (Ruth 2:13 MSG).

Ruth left with fifty pounds of grain and a smile she couldn't wipe off her face. Naomi heard the story and recognized, first the name, then the opportunity, saying, "Boaz... Boaz... that name sounds familiar. He's Rahab's boy! He was the freckle-faced tornado at the family reunions. Ruth, he's one of our cousins!"

Naomi's head began to spin with possibilities. She motioned for her daughter-in-law to slide her chair near and listen carefully. This being harvest season, Boaz would be eating dinner with the men and spending the night on the threshing floor to protect the crop from intruders. So she instructed Ruth to wash and perfume herself, and put on her best clothes, sneak down to the threshing floor, and after Boaz is lying down to uncover his feet and lie down next to him and wait for Boaz to tell her what to do next.

Pardon me while I wipe the steam off my glasses! How did this midnight, Moabite advance get into the Bible? Boaz, full-bellied and sleepy. Ruth bathed and perfumed. Uncover his feet and lie down. What was Naomi thinking?

She was thinking it was time for Ruth to get on with her life. Ruth was still grieving the death of her husband. When Naomi told her to "put on your best clothes," she used a phrase that describes a robe of mourning. As long as she was dressed in black, Boaz, respectable man he was, would keep his distance. New clothing signaled Ruth's re-entrance into society. Naomi was also thinking about the law of the kinsman-redeemer. This intricate custom accomplished two goals: protection of land and provision for childless widows. If a man died without children, his property was transferred, not to his wife, but to his nearest living relative. This practice kept the land in the clan. But it also left the widow vulnerable. To protect her, the law required the brother of the deceased to marry the childless widow. It was grace in action.

If the deceased husband had no brother, his nearest relative was to provide for the widow but not necessarily marry her. This law kept the property in the family, gave the widow protection, and, in some cases, a husband.

In the case of Naomi and Ruth, they had no children, but they had a distant cousin named Boaz who had already been kind to them once. Maybe he would be again. It was worth the gamble. According to Ruth 3:7–8 (NIV):

[Ruth] went down to the threshing floor and _____ her mother-in-law told her to do. When Boaz had finished eating and drinking and was in good spirits, he went over to lie down at the far end of the grain pile.

Ruth lingered in the shadows, watching the men sit around the fire and finish their meals. One by one, they stood and wandered off to bed, down for the night. Laughter and chatter gave way to snores of slumber. Soon the threshing floor was quiet. By the light of the still popping fire, Ruth made her move. She crept through the lumps of sleeping men in the direction of Boaz. Upon reaching him, she

_____ and lay down. In the middle of the night something startled the man; he turned--and there was a woman lying at his feet!_____ (Ruth 3:6–8 NIV).

Startled, indeed! This was a gesture roughly equivalent to the giving of an engagement ring.

"I am _____ Ruth," she said. "Spread the corner of your garment over me, since you are a _____" (Ruth 3:9 NIV).

Audacious move. Who was she but a foreigner? Who was he but Boaz, the prominent landowner? She was a destitute alien. He was a local powerbroker. She, unknown. He, well-known.

She fragile.

He forceful.

She—you.

He—God.

By now you have noticed, Ruth's story is ours. We too are poor. We hail from enemy lands wearing robes of death. But our Boaz has taken note of us. Just as the landowner came to Ruth, "while we were yet sinners," Christ came to us (Romans 5:8). He made the first move. And we responded. We cast ourselves at the feet of God. And thanks to the kindness of Christ, we have become the bride of Christ. Think about this wonderful promise of God.

The LORD will _____ those who _____ him (Psalm 34:22 NLT).

We are the modern-day version of Ruth. Ruth shared life with Boaz. She moved into the ranch house. Naomi occupied the guest villa. Boaz traded his Mercedes convertible for a minivan and his poker night for family night. Last glance had Boaz, Ruth, and Naomi posing for a family photo with their brand-new baby boy, Obed, who later went on to raise a son named Jesse, who fathered David, the second most famous king to be born in Bethlehem. You know the most famous king—Jesus. Now you know Him as even more: your kinsman-redeemer. The story that began with two widows and grief concludes with the promise of Christ and life.

This sort of thing happens when God makes a promise. This sort of thing happens when we trust Him to keep it. God promises to redeem you. So take that promise to heart by making your own promise.

My promise: I will turn to Christ, my kinsman-redeemer.

QUESTIONS FOR REFLECTION:

1. What does it mean to be "redeemed"?

_____

_____

_____

_____

2. How do we accept God's redemption?

_____

_____

_____

_____

_____

3. When have you embraced the promise that Jesus is your kinsman-redeemer?

_____

_____

_____

_____

_____

CHAPTER ELEVEN:

THE BATTLE IS THE LORD'S

I spent a better part of an hour recently reciting to my wife the woes of my life. I felt overwhelmed by commitments and deadlines. I had been sick with the flu. There was tension at the church between some of my friends. We would received word of a couple who were getting a divorce. And then, to top it off, I received a manuscript from my editor that was bloody with red ink. I actually looked for a chapter that did not need a re-write. There was not one. (Groan.)

After several minutes listening to my ranting, Denalyn interrupted me with a question: "Is God in this anywhere?" I just hate it when she does that. I was not thinking about God. I was not consulting God. I was not turning to God. I was not talking about God.

Maybe you have been there. You have had a hard week at work. Your project is not going well, and your boss does not seem to notice how many late nights you are putting in. Nothing seems to be going right. All you can do is lie awake at night in the few hours you are able squeeze in and worry about the next day. You eat, sleep, and dream the problem.

The question comes—is God in this anywhere?

Your marriage is coming apart at the seams. Harsh comments and resentful replies are the common thread woven through each interaction. You only see two options: live this way forever or cut the tie. The question returns: is God in this anywhere?

The bills on your desk tower like a house of cards about to topple. Worry and fear grip your heart. Frustration and stress take you to places you do not want to go. Again the question is asked: is God in this anywhere?

When you are facing a battle that seems too big to win—maybe even impossible—there is a powerful promise for you to consider in 1 Samuel 17:47 (NIV):

All those gathered here will know that it is not by sword or spear that _____; for _____ is the Lord's, and he will give all of you into our hands.

Sometimes it feels like we are in a constant battle. A battle for our heart, a battle for our relationships, a battle for our finances, a battle for our peace. It can be exhausting and overwhelming. But we were never meant to fight our battles alone.

In Matthew 1:23, God called Himself "Immanuel"—which means *God with us*! Not just God who made us; not just God who thinks about us; not just God above us; God...with...us! He breathed our air and walked this earth.

He pressed His fingers into the sore of the leper. He felt the tears of the sinful woman who wept. He inclined His ear to the cry of the hungry. He wept at the death of a friend. He stopped His work to tend to the needs of a grieving mother. He does not recoil, run, or retreat at the sight of pain. Just the opposite. He walks with us through it. He did not walk the earth in an insulated bubble or preach from an isolated, germ-free, pain-free island. He came into our mess to show us a way out. He stepped on to the battlefield and showed us how to win.

In some of the biggest wars in history, were it not for the allies and reinforcements that came in, the battles would have been lost. Jesus is stronger than any natural reinforcement and He has already won the final war. When we are facing insurmountable odds, when the battle looks hopeless, when we are weary from the fight, we are not alone. We have the ultimate Victor on our side, and we can walk through the battle knowing it has already been won.

Is God in this anywhere? He certainly is. And we must acknowledge His authority. We must allow Him to show us the battle plan, to teach us how to fight the good fight, and ultimately, let Him be the one on the frontlines fighting for us.

Jesus said in John 16:33 (NIV):

"I have told you these things, so that_____ you may have peace. In the world you will _____. But take heart! I have _____ the world."

How do we have peace in the midst of the battles raging around us? We take heart and realize that He has already overcome them. He has a plan and WE are overcomers because of Jesus. The One who has overcome the world is there to fight the battle. You are not alone. Take heart.

Whatever you are walking through. Whatever battle you are facing right now. Whatever the unlikeliness of the victory, remember the battle is the Lord's.

GOD'S PROMISE:

The battle is the Lord's.

MY PROMISE:

I will battle in the name of the Lord Almighty.

You may have thought the battle was yours to fight, yours to win or lose, yours to sustain. It is not. "The battle is the Lord's." Thank you, David, for modeling this promise.

Not King David. Not Royal David. But, young, shepherd-boy David. Mud moistens his knees. Bubbling water cools his hand. Were he to notice, he could study his handsome features in the water. Hair the color of copper. Tanned, ruddy skin and eyes that steal the breath of Hebrew maidens. He searches not for his reflection, however, but for rocks. Stones. Smooth stones. The kind that stack neatly in a shepherd's pouch, rest flush against a shepherd's leather sling. Flat rocks that balance heavy on the palm and missile with comet-crashing force into the head of a lion, a bear, or, in this case, a giant.

Goliath stares down from the hillside. Only disbelief keeps him from laughing. He and his Philistine herd have rendered their half of the valley into a forest of spears; a growling, bloodthirsty gang of hoodlums boasting rotten teeth and barbed-wire tattoos. Goliath towers above them all: nine feet, nine inches tall in his stocking feet, wearing 125 pounds of armor, and snarling like the main contender at the World Wrestling Entertainment championship night. He wears a size 20 collar, a 10½ hat, and a 56-inch belt. His biceps burst, thigh muscles ripple, and boasts belch through the canyon:

"This day I _____! Give me a man and let us _____ each other" (1 Samuel 17:10 NIV).

Who will go *mano a mano conmigo*?

No Hebrew answered.

Until today.

Until David.

David just showed up this morning. He clocked out of sheep watching where he was usually found to deliver bread and cheese to his brothers on the battlefront. And that's when David makes his decision. He selects five smooth stones.

Goliath scoffs at the kid, nicknames him Twiggy.

"Am I a _____, that you come to me with _____?" (1 Samuel 17:43 NASB).

What odds do you give David against his giant? Better odds, perhaps, than you give yourself against yours.

Your Goliath does not carry sword or shield; he brandishes blades of unemployment, abandonment, abuse, or depression. You know well the roar of Goliath. The regretful taunting of your past, the mocking dread about your future. The unrelenting, fear-filled questions about your present. His voice is defiant and uncompassionate. Meant to terrorize and paralyze you,

But on this day, David faced one who foghorned his challenges morning and night. Scripture says that:

For _____,every, morning and evening, th_____ strutted in front of the Israelite army (1 Samuel 17:16 NLT).

Yours does the same. First thought of the morning, last worry of the night—your Goliath dominates your day, contaminates your hope, infuriates your soul, and infiltrates your joy. Goliath: the bully of the valley. Tougher than a two-dollar steak.

But not tougher than David's God. When David saw the giant, David said this:

"What will be done for the man who _____ this Philistine and _____ from Israel? Who is this uncircumcised Philistine that he should _____ of the living God?" (1 Samuel 17:26 NIV)

He called Goliath a name—"Uncircumcised Philistine," or in modern parlance, "filthy, rotten scoundrel." Politically correct? No. But spiritually aware. David marched into the battle keenly aware of the "...armies of the living God."

He saw a battle; he thought of God.

He saw the Philistine armies; he thought of God's armies.

David majored in God. He saw the giant, mind you; he just saw God more so. Look carefully at David's battle cry:

"You come against me with _____ and _____ and _____. But I come against you in the _____, the God of the armies of Israel" (1 Samuel 17:45 NIV).

Note the plural noun—*armies* of Israel. Armies? The common observer sees only one army of Israel. Not David. He saw the Allies on D-day: platoons of angels and infantries of saints, the weapons of the wind and the forces of the earth. God could pelt the enemy with hail as He did for Moses, collapse walls as He did for Joshua, stir thunder as He did for Samuel.

David saw the armies of God.

And because he did, David hurried and ran toward the army to meet the Philistine.

David's brothers covered their eyes, both in fear and embarrassment. Saul sighed as the young Hebrew raced to certain death. Goliath threw back his head in laughter, just enough to shift his helmet and expose a square inch of forehead flesh. David spotted the target and seized the moment. The sound of the swirling sling was the only sound in the valley.

Ssshhhww. Ssshhhww. Ssshhhww.

The stone torpedoed into the skull; Goliath's eyes crossed and legs buckled. He crumpled to the ground and died. David ran over and yanked Goliath's sword from its sheath, shish-kebabed the Philistine, and cut off his head.

You might say that David knew how to get a *head* of his giant.

When was the last time you did the same? How long since you ran toward your challenge? We tend to retreat, duck behind a desk of work, or crawl into a nightclub of distraction, or a bed of forbidden love. For a moment, a day, or a year, we feel safe, insulated, anesthetized, but then the work runs out, the liquor wears off, or the lover leaves, and we hear Goliath again.

Booming.

Bombastic.

It is like the armor that King Saul tried to offer David. A shield for David to hide behind, armor to cover him. But these attempts at protection were just that—only fatal attempts. David had to change his tactic. He had to face the giant head on. No hiding. No trying to pretend like he was someone he was not. No false display of bravery while shaking in his boots. He had to stand on the promises of God and face Goliath with boldness.

And he took down that giant. It is time we do the same.

Like David, rush your giant with a God-saturated soul. Amplify God and minimize Goliath. Download some of heaven's unshakable resolve. *Giant of divorce, you are not entering my home! Giant of depression? It may take a lifetime, but you won't conquer me. Giant of alcohol, bigotry, abuse, insecurity ...you are going down.* How long since you loaded your sling and took a swing at your giant?

Too long, you say? Then David is your model. God called him "a man after my own heart" (Acts 13:22 NIV). He gave the appellation to no one else. Not Abraham or Moses or Joseph. He called Paul an apostle, John his beloved, but neither was tagged a man after God's own heart.

It is not just you and Goliath. You are not alone in your struggles. Lay claim to this great and powerful promise. The next time you hear the bully of the valley snort and strut, you remind yourself and him of the promise in 1 Samuel 17:47: "This battle belongs to the Lord." And then with a boldness like David's, make your own promise:

I will battle in the name of the Lord Almighty!

QUESTIONS FOR REFLECTION:

1. Name the biggest giant you are facing right now. Marital difficulties? A financial crisis? A scary report from your doctor? Give your giant a name.

_____

_____

_____

_____

2. Remember, this battle belongs to the Lord. How does this promise affect your thoughts, your words, your actions?

_____

_____

_____

_____

3. What are five smooth stones you can use to defeat the giants in your life?

_____

_____

_____

_____

PRAYING THE PROMISE:

Lord, You are the slayer of giants,
the God whose angelic army is able to defeat any foe I might face.
My battle is not against flesh and blood, but against the enemy of my soul.
An enemy You have conquered.
By Your grace help me to trust that the battle truly is Yours.
Let me go forth in praise and trust,
believing You can and will defeat all of my giants.
Amen.

CHAPTER TWELVE:

GREAT THINGS HAPPEN WHEN WE PRAY

I accompanied Denalyn on some errand-running recently. We stopped at an office supply store so she could buy a calendar. As we walked through the parking lot, I pointed at the sign and said: "Honey, this is my store. OfficeMAX!"

She was unimpressed.

I hurried to the front door and held it open. "Come into MY store."

She rolled her eyes. I used to think that the "rolling of the eyes" was a gesture of frustration.

After thirty-five years I now realize it is a symbol of admiration! After all, she does it so often. I continued my posturing as we shopped, thanking her for coming to "my" store to buy product off of "my" shelves.

She just rolled her eyes at me again. I think she was speechless. When we reached the checkout line, I told the clerk my status.

I arched an eyebrow and deepened my voice. "Hi, I am Max." She smiled and proceeded to ring up the sale.

"As in *OfficeMax*."

She looked at me, then Denalyn. Denalyn rolled her eyes again. Such admiration for her husband. I was beginning to blush.

"I am the boss of this place."

"Really?" she looked at me with no smile.

"Why don't you just take the afternoon off?" I asked.

"What?"

"Take the afternoon off. If anyone asks, tell them that Max of *OfficeMax* told them to go home."

This time she stopped and looked at me: "Sir, you may have the name, but you do not have the clout."

Well, she was right about me, but the same cannot be said about you. If you have taken on the name of Christ, then you do have clout. When you speak, God listens. When you pray, heaven takes note. What you bind on earth is bound in heaven. What you loose on earth is loosed in heaven. Your prayer impacts the actions of God. James 5:16 in the New Living Translation says:

The _____ of a righteous person has great power and produces _____.

And according to 2 Corinthians 5:21 (NIV):

For God made Christ, _____, to be the offering for our sin, so that we could _____ with God through Christ.

Let that sink in. The prayers of a righteous person are powerful. God has made you righteous!

Your prayers are powerful! According to Scripture, they produce wonderful results!

A dramatic illustration of this promise is found among the Christians of Russia. For eight decades of the twentieth century, Christians in Russia experienced systematic persecution from the communist government. School teachers would hold up a Bible and ask students if they had seen such a book in their homes. If a student said yes, a government official would visit the family. Pastors and lay people were imprisoned, never to be heard from again. The Soviet Gulag required pastors to visit their offices once a week to report on any new visitors. Sermon topics had to be approved.

This was the world in which a man named Dmitri practiced his faith. He and his family lived in a small village, four hours from Moscow. The nearest church was a three-day walk, making it impossible for them to attend church more than twice a year.

Dmitri began to teach his family Bible stories and verses. Neighbors got wind of the lessons and wanted to participate. Within a short time, the group grew to twenty-five people. Officials took notice and demanded he stop. He refused. When the groups reached fifty people, Dmitri was dismissed from his factory job and his wife was fired from her teaching position. His sons were expelled from school.

Still he continued.

When the gathering increased to seventy-five people, there was not enough room in his house. Villagers squeezed into every available corner and closed in around the windows so they might listen to this man of God teach. One night, a group of soldiers burst into the gathering. A soldier grabbed Dmitri and slapped him back and forth across the face. He then warned the people to stop or the same would happen to them.

As the officer turned to leave, a small grandmother stepped in his path and waved a finger in his face. "You have laid hands on a man of God and you will NOT survive."

Within two days the officer was dead from a heart attack.

The fear of God spread and 150 people showed up for the next house meeting. Dmitri was arrested and sentenced to seventeen years in prison. His jail cell was so small that he needed only one step to reach each wall. He was the only believer among fifteen hundred prisoners. The officials tortured him and the prisoners mocked him. Yet, he never broke. Each morning at daybreak, Dmitri stood attention by his bed, faced eastward, raised his arms to God, and sang a song of praise. Other prisoners would jeer, still he sang.

Whenever he found a piece of scrap paper, he scribbled a verse or story from memory. When the paper was completely filled, he took it to the corner of his cell and affixed it to a damp pillar as a sacrifice to Jesus. Officials routinely spotted the papers, removed them, and beat Dmitri. Still, he worshipped.

This went on for seventeen years. Only on one occasion did he nearly recant his faith. Guards convinced him that his wife had been murdered and his children were wards of the state.

The thought was more than Dmitri could bear. He agreed to renounce his faith in Christ. The guards told him that they would return the next day with a document. All he had to do was sign it and he would be released.

The officials were sure of their victory. What they did not know was this: when believing people pray, great things happen.

Believing people were praying for Dmitri. A thousand kilometers away, that night, his family sensed a special burden to pray for him. They knelt in a circle and interceded passionately for his protection. Miraculously, the Lord allowed Dmitri to hear the voices of his loved ones as they prayed.

He knew they were safe.

The next morning, when the guards came for his signature, they saw a renewed man. His face was calm and his eyes were resolute. "I am not signing anything," he told them. "In the night, God let me hear the voices of my wife and my children and my brother praying for me. You lied to me! I know that my wife is alive and physically well. I know that my sons are with her. I know that they are all still in Christ. So I am not signing anything!"

The officials beat and threatened to execute him, but Dmitri's resolve only increased. He still worshipped in the mornings and posted verses on the pillar. Finally, the authorities had all they could take. They dragged Dmitri from his cell through the corridor in the center of the prison toward the place of execution. As they did, fifteen hundred criminals raised their hands and began to sing the song of praise they had heard Dmitri sing each morning.

The jailers released their hold on him and stepped back. "Who are you?"

"I am a son of the living God, and Jesus is His name." Dmitri was returned to his cell. Sometime later he was released and returned to his family.

You'll likely never find yourself in a Russian prison, but you may find yourself in an impossible situation. You'll feel outnumbered and outmaneuvered. You will want to quit. Could I ask you, implore you, to memorize this promise and ask God to bring it to mind on that day? Write it where you will find it. Tattoo it, if not on your skin, at least on your heart:

When a _____ prays, great things happen (James 5:16 NCV).

GOD'S PROMISE:

When you pray in faith, I will answer.

MY PROMISE:

I will make prayer my priority and passion.

Prayer is a powerful catalyst of change. For proof, consider the story of Elijah. He lived during one of the darkest days in the history of Israel. The Northern Kingdom had nineteen kings, each one of whom was evil.

Ahab was one of the most evil kings in Israel's history. Influenced by his wife, he turned from the God of Israel to serve pagan gods, and ruled the people in wickedness and cruelty. The Bible even says:

No one else so _____ to what was evil in the Lord's sight as Ahab did under the influence of his wife Jezebel (1 Kings 21:25–26 NIV).

Ahab would not turn from his evil ways so an ultimatum was given to him through the prophet. The name Elijah means "My God is Jehovah," and he lived up to his name. He gave King Ahab an unsolicited weather report. In 1 Kings 17:1 (NIV) he tells the king:

"As the LORD, the God of Israel, lives, _____,
there will be neither dew nor rain in the next few years except
_____."

Elijah's attack was calibrated. Baal was the fertility god of the pagans,
the god to whom they looked for rain and fertile fields. Elijah called for a
showdown: the true God of Israel against the false god of the pagans. How
could Elijah be so confident of the impending drought?

Because he had prayed.

Eight centuries later, the prayers of Elijah were used as a model by James,
one of Jesus' disciples. In chapter 5, verses 16–18 (NCV) James wrote:

When a believing person _____, great things happen. Elijah
was a human being just like us. He _____ that it would not rain,
and it did not rain on the land for three and a half years! Then Elijah
_____, and the rain came down from the sky, and the land
produced crops again.

James was impressed that a prayer of such power came from a person so
common. Elijah was "a human being, even as we are" but his prayers were
heard because he prayed, not eloquently but earnestly. This was no casual
prayer or comfortable prayer, but a radical prayer. "Do whatever it takes,
Lord," Elijah begged, "even if that means no water."

So Ahab sent word throughout all Israel and assembled the prophets on
Mount Carmel. Elijah went before the people and said:

"How long will you _____?
If the LORD is God, follow him; but if Baal is God, follow him." But the
people _____ (1 Kings 18:20-21 NIV).

The word "waver" is the exact Hebrew word used later for "dance" (vs. 26). *How long are you going to do this dance? You dance with God, then Baal; how long will this continue?*

What happens next is one of the greatest stories in the Bible. Elijah told the 450 prophets of Baal: *You get a bull; I will get a bull. You build an altar; I will build an altar. You ask your God to send fire, I will ask my God to send fire. The God who answers by fire is the true God.* The prophets of Baal agreed and went first.

At noon Elijah began to taunt them. "Shout louder!" he said. "Surely he is a god! Perhaps he is deep in thought, or busy, or traveling. Maybe he is sleeping and must be awakened." So they tried harder and shouted louder and begged and pleaded. They resorted to cutting themselves as was the custom. Midday passed, and they continued their frantic prophesying until it was time for the evening sacrifice. (See 1 Kings 18:27–29.)

The prophet continued to taunt them. Elijah would have flunked a course in diplomacy. Though the prophets cut themselves and raved all afternoon, nothing happened. It says, "There was no response, no one answered, no one paid attention." Their god was silent. Finally, Elijah asked for his turn.

He called everyone close and the crowd gathered round. Then Elijah prayed this powerful prayer:

"Lord, the God of Abraham, Isaac and Israel, let it be known today that you are _____ and that I am _____ and have done all these things at _____. Answer me, Lord, answer me, so these people will know that you, Lord, are God, and that you are _____ back again" (1 Kings 18:36–37 NIV).

Note how quickly God answered.

The next verse says,

Then the _____ fell and burned up the sacrifice, the wood, the stones and the soil, and also licked up the water in the trench. When all the people saw this, they fell prostrate and cried, "_____" (1 Kings 18:38–39 NIV).

No request for fire was made, just the heart of the prophet was revealed and *pow!* the altar was ablaze. God delighted in Elijah's prayer. God delights in yours as well.

You are never without hope because you are never without prayer. But *why*, we wonder. Why would our prayers matter? We cannot get the plumber to call us back; why would God listen to our ideas? Simple. Your prayers matter to God because you matter to God. You are not just anybody; you are His child.

God longs to be asked for what He longs to give.

Will He do what we want? Sometimes and sometimes not. But even when He says "no," He says "yes." He may not like our idea, but He still likes us. He loves to be asked for help. Let your prayers be heard.

He will hear yours as well.

Remember the promise in James 5:16:

When a believing person prays, great things happen (James 5:16 NCV).

God loves bold prayers, and just as He delighted in and answered Elijah's prayers, He will answer ours as well.

So let's make this our promise: **I will make prayer my priority and passion.**

QUESTIONS FOR REFLECTION:

1. We read in James 5:16 that the prayers of a righteous person produce great results. Are you righteous? Why or why not?

_____

_____

_____

_____

2. What made Elijah's prayers different from those of the prophets of Baal?

_____

_____

_____

_____

3. How will you make prayer a priority and a passion in your life? What steps can you take today?

_____

_____

_____

_____

_____

Chapter Thirteen:

God Gives Grace to the Humble

When he was not flying his private jet across the Atlantic or watching sunsets from the deck of one of his yachts, he was living a life of luxury inside his ten-thousand-square-foot Lexington Avenue Penthouse in New York City.

His yacht cost seven million dollars. His jet cost twenty-four million. He had a home in France, a beach home in Montauk, and a house in Palm Beach. He had boats and cars. His wife had furs and designer handbags, Wedgwood china, and Christofle silver. When it came to décor, she spared no expense. Gold sconces lined the wallpaper. Central Asian rugs covered the floors. Greek and

Egyptian statues competed for the approval of guests.

Everyone wanted to know him. People stood in line to shake his hand, people like Stephen Spielberg and Elie Wiesel. To stand in his Manhattan office was to stand in the epicenter of investment success.

Or so it seemed.

And then came the morning of December 10, 2008. That's when the charade ended. That's when Bernie Madoff knew he had been caught. That's when this generation's most infamous scam artist sat down with his wife and two sons and confessed, "It's all a lie. It was a giant Ponzi scheme."

Over the next days, weeks, and months the staggering details became public knowledge.

Madoff had masterminded a twenty-year-long shell game, the largest financial crime in US history. He had swindled people, rich and poor alike, out of billions of dollars.

His collapse was of biblical proportions. Within short order he was stripped of everything. No money. No future. No family. One of his sons committed suicide. The other changed his last name. His wife went into seclusion. And seventy-four-year-old Bernie Madoff was sentenced to spend the rest of his life as prisoner number 61727054 in the Federal Correction complex of Butner, North Carolina.

Why did he do it? What makes a man live a lie for decades? What was the trade-off for Madoff?

In a word, stature.

According to one biographer, "He was spurned and humiliated as a kid for...his inferior intellect...rejected by one girl after another...relegated to lesser classes and lesser schools...but he excelled at making money, and with it came the stature that had once eluded him."

Stature. Madoff was addicted to adulation. He was hooked on recognition. He wanted the applause of people, and money was his way of earning it. He elbowed and clawed his way to the top of the mountain only to discover that its peak is greasy and crowded.

If only he had known this promise:

God resists the _____, but he gives grace to the _____ (1 Peter 5:5 NIV).

Pride is deceptive, is it not? It gives tunnel vision so that we see everything through the lens of "me." Our focus is on self. The self-centered see everything through self. Their motto? "It's all about me!" The flight schedule, the traffic, the dress styles, the worship styles, the weather, the work—everything is filtered through the mini-ME in the eye. We think we are bigger than life and know more than others.

God resists pride. But He uses those who walk in humility. He loves humility. Jesus told His followers, "Blessed are the humble, for they shall inherit the earth." God can do so much through someone who has a humble heart before Him.

Some time ago I partnered with musician Michael W. Smith for a ministry weekend at a beautiful facility owned by the Billy Graham Association. A few hours before the event, Michael and I met to go over the weekend schedule. But Michael was so moved by what he had just experienced that he hardly discussed the retreat. He had just met with Billy Graham for the purpose of planning Reverend Graham's funeral. The famous evangelist was, at the time, ninety-four years old. He was confined to a wheelchair, on oxygen. His mind was sharp and spirits were high. But his body was seeing its final days. So he called for Michael. And he called for his pastor. He wanted to discuss his funeral. He told them that he had one request.

"Whatever you want," they assured him.

His request? "Would you not mention my name?" "What?"

"Can you not mention my name? Just mention the name of Jesus."

Billy Graham preached to more than a billion people. He filled stadiums on every continent. He advised nearly every president of the last half century. He was consistently at the top of every most-admired list. Yet, he wanted to be unmentioned at his own funeral. He wanted all the honor and attention to go to God. That was a man of humility, a man who put God's kingdom first.

He is a picture of the promise God makes to us all. First Peter 5:5 is a call to humility:

God resists the _____, but he gives grace to the _____.

GOD'S PROMISE:

I reward humility.

MY PROMISE:

I will pursue humility.

The earthly kingdoms will come and go. Human enterprises will rise and fall. The endeavors of mankind will seem to last forever, but they won't. God's kingdom, however, is an everlasting kingdom. In 609 BC, King Nebuchadnezzar overthrew Jerusalem, taking many Hebrews into captivity. Among his Hebrew captives was a young man named Daniel, and his three friends Shadrach, Meshach and Abednego.

The Bible says that Daniel purposed in his heart not to go down the same path as those around him, and he encouraged his friends to do likewise. He was honoring to those in authority over him, but stood strong for what he believed. Though he was a slave in the natural, they could not chain or change his spirit. Daniel 5:3 (NIV) tells us:

He had favor because he was _____ and had an _____. Those in authority took notice and he began to gain _____ from all who knew him.

King Nebuchadnezzar could have taken a lesson from this young Hebrew boy.

The king was quite full of himself. So much so that he built a ninety-foot tall golden statue of *himself*, in *his* honor, and commanded the people to bow down before it. Talk about an ego! The Jewish boys refused to bow to any God but theirs, so the king heated the furnace to seven times its normal heat and threw them into the fire. When they came out not even smelling of smoke, he was amazed. But did King Nebuchadnezzar humble himself?

Sadly, no.

Twenty or thirty years passed. Nebuchadnezzar was enjoying a time of peace and prosperity. The city of Babylon was immense. His enemies were at bay. His wealth was secure. Yet, in the midst of all this, he had a dream. His fortune-tellers could not explain it, so he called on Daniel, who had interpreted his dreams in the past:

He told Daniel that in his dream he had seen an enormous tree touching the sky. A beautiful, fruit-filled tree giving shelter to all the animals and birds in the land. He went on to describe how a messenger from heaven cut down the tree. Its branches were trimmed and fruit scattered. Only a stump remained. The voice from heaven then made a pronouncement:

"Let him be drenched with the dew of heaven, and let him live with the

animals among the plants of the earth. Let his _____

from that of a man and let him be given the _____,

till seven times pass by for him" (Daniel 4:10–16 NIV).

Daniel listened to the dream and gulped. He was astonished and troubled by what he heard. Daniel told him:

"Your Majesty, _____ are that tree!... You will be driven away _____ and will live with the wild animals; you will eat grass like the ox and be drenched with the dew of heaven. Seven times will pass by for you until you acknowledge that _____ over all kingdoms on earth and gives them to anyone he wishes. The command to leave the stump of the tree with its roots means that your kingdom will be restored to you when you _____ that heaven rules" (Daniel 4:22–26 NIV).

Nebuchadnezzar thought he was in charge. He believed that he ran his world, perhaps the whole world. No kingdom was greater than his! No king greater than him! His dream was intended to teach him that the Most High God was sovereign over all the kingdoms on earth, and it was He who could raise up and take down kings and kingdoms.

Daniel urged the king to repent so that his kingdom and prosperity could continue. But did Nebuchadnezzar change?

Twelve months later, as the king was walking on the roof of the royal palace of Babylon, he looked at the kingdom around him and bombastically proclaimed:

"Is not this the great Babylon that _____ have built as the royal residence, by _____ and for the glory of

_____?" (Daniel 4:29 NIV)

Oh, the proliferation of pronouns. "*I* have built...*my* power...*my* majesty." The king was all about the king. God had given the king a year to climb down from his pompous throne. It was obvious he had remained unmoved from his arrogant and prideful position. But a throne built on a foundation of pride is a shaky and dangerous one.

Daniel chapter 4, verse 30 (NIV), tells it this way:

Even as the words were on his lips, a voice _____, "This is what is decreed for you, King Nebuchadnezzar: Your _____ has been taken from you. You will be driven away from people and will live with the wild animals; you will eat grass like the ox."

The king became an ancient version of Howard Hughes: corkscrew fingernails, wild hair, animalistic. When the mighty fall, the fall is mighty. One minute he was on the cover of *Time* magazine, the next he was banished like a caged creature. And we are left with a lesson: *God hates pride.*

Proverbs 26:12 (NIV) tells us:

Do you see a person _____ in their own eyes? There is more hope _____ than him.

God resists the proud because the proud resist God. Arrogance stiffens the knee so it will not kneel, hardens the heart so it will not admit to sin. Pride is the hidden reef that shipwrecks the soul. Pride not only prevents salvation from God, it prevents reconciliation with people. How many marriages have collapsed beneath the weight of foolish pride? How many apologies have gone unoffered, born of the lack of humility? How many wars have sprouted from the rocky soil of arrogance?

Pride comes at a high price. Do not pay it.

Choose instead to stand on the offer of grace.

To the degree that God hates arrogance, He loves humility. Is it not easy to see why? Humility is happy to do what pride will not. The humble heart is quick to acknowledge the need for God, glad to confess sin, willing to kneel before heaven's mighty hand.

Daniel was one of these men. No promise of success, no threat of death, could move him from his posture of humility before God.

God came first.

King Nebuchadnezzar finally learned this lesson. It took seven years, but he got the point.

At the end of that time Nebuchadnezzar, raised his eyes towards heaven, and his sanity was restored. Then he praised God, declaring:

"Now I, Nebuchadnezzar, _____ the King of heaven, because everything he does is right and all his ways are just. And those who _____ he is able to _____" (Daniel 4:37 NIV).

The king finally learned what Daniel understood: God resists the proud but gives grace to the humble.

You and I can be like Daniel, as we answer God's promise to us with our own promise:

"I will pursue humility."

QUESTIONS FOR REFLECTION:

1. Why do you think pride is such a grave sin in the eyes of God?

_____

_____

_____

_____

_____

_____

2. How would you define humility? How do you spot a humble person?

_____

_____

_____

_____

_____

3. What is your biggest challenge in pursuing humility?

_____

_____

_____

_____

_____

CHAPTER FOURTEEN:

GOD WORKS ALL THINGS FOR GOOD

The character's name is Bernie Lootz. In the movie, Bernie, nicknamed "the Cooler," is the most unlucky guy in the world. Nothing goes his way. He lives in a dreary, run-down, flea-bitten motel near the Las Vegas strip. He has so much bad luck that a casino manager hires him to be a "cooler." His job is to find gamblers who are on a hot streak and let the aura of his bad luck rub off on them.

It worked.

A fellow at the card table is on a run, making a fortune. He goes stone cold once Bernie shows up. Poker players on a hot streak suddenly start getting bad cards when "Mr. Cooler" appears.

Shelley, his friend and casino manager, calls Bernie the "walking kryptonite."

Maybe you feel like Bernie. Life is like a bad night in Vegas. Your destiny is left to the roll of the dice and nothing is falling your way. No lucky sevens, no snake eyes, no boxcars. You cannot get that break. The committee is considering renaming Murphy's Law after you. You did not get the job. You always choose the wrong lane. You did not get the girl. You are always in the wrong place at the wrong time. Your buttered bread always falls face down. You constantly feel like the kid who just missed the bus.

Have you ever had a situation that did not go the way you expected? It did not look like anything good could come out of it? Well I have an amazing promise for you:

...in all things God works for the _____ of those who love him (Romans 8:28 NIV).

My friend Roy was sitting on a park bench one morning as he watched a little guy struggling to get on the school bus that stopped just a few feet away. He was leaning down frantically trying to "un-knot" a knotted shoestring. All of a sudden it was too late—the door was closing. The little boy fell back on his haunches and sighed. Then he saw Roy. Tears in his eyes, he looked at the man on the bench and asked, "Do you untie knots?"

Sometimes it just feels like life is filled with mean, mangled "knots," does not it? You are NOT going to get out of this stuck place you are in. You are NOT getting the promotion. You are NOT accepted into the program. You did NOT make the team. You do NOT belong here. What NOTS are holding you down?

Jesus loves the request of that little boy. Life gets tangled. We get stuck. We miss the bus. But Jesus has a way of appearing in such moments to untangle the knots of impossible predicaments.

Peter's boat was empty.

Lazarus was six feet under.

The disciples had seven thousand people to feed and one basket of bread and fish.

Look who just so happened to show up...Jesus!

Have you ever noticed all the "just so happened" moments in the Bible?

Joseph *just so happened* to end up in the same cell with the man who could plead his case to the king. Ruth *just so happened* to gather wheat from the field of Boaz, the man who could redeem her family. David *just so happened* to be sent to the battlefield when Goliath was making his threats. The fish Peter caught *just so happened* to have a coin in its mouth to pay the taxes, as Jesus said it would. And Jesus *just so happened* to rise from the dead on the third day after His crucifixion, exactly as Scripture foretold.

In all of these scenarios, things weren't going so well until God showed up on the scene. But that's the God we serve. The One who can reach down and untangle our knots no matter how mangled they may be.

We all walk through dark seasons. Seasons that sometimes cannot be explained. Asking why is futile. Asking how long is pointless. But there IS one shining light of revelation in this dark place.

David addressed it in Psalm 23:

**Though I walk through the _____,
I will fear no evil, for _____ (NIV).**

We may not see why we are walking through this season. We may not know how long the path is to the light at the other end. But what we do know is that He is with us.

We are not walking it alone. We are not left to trudge through the messy places by ourselves. No, there is One who has walked the path before us and knows the way. He steps in and walks with us through it to the other side. And, I might add, is great company along the way! Encouraging us, teaching us, and strengthening us.

GOD'S PROMISE:

I will work all things for good for those who love Me.

This gives us unshakable hope through every season, that no matter what we are walking through, we can be confident He will work it for good.

MY PROMISE:

I will do what is right and trust God for the outcome.

It was the fifth century BC. The city was Susa, the capital city of the Persian Empire. The Israelites had been living in the area for more than one hundred years. Once prisoners, they now were free.

And here we find a beautiful young Hebrew girl named Esther. She was orphaned as a young girl and raised by her uncle Mordecai. She would soon have the leading role in an unfolding story of prejudice, heroism, and sacrifice.

The villain of this story is Haman. Haman despised the Israelites who were spread throughout the 127 provinces of the Persian Empire. But he had it out for one particular Israelite who refused to bow down to him when he passed: Esther's uncle, Mordecai.

Haman went to King Xerxes and convinced him that the Israelites were bad people who needed to be eliminated in the best interest of the kingdom. He suggested that the king issue an official decree giving permission for the Persians to kill any Hebrew they came across on one specific day. To give incentive for such violence, the Persians could keep all the possessions of the family they destroyed. It was legalized lynching and looting.

The king went along with the idea, sealing the deal with his signet ring pressed into hot wax. It was an irreversible plan. Not even the king could change it now. Haman was going to have his revenge.

Yet, there was another storyline developing that would eventually collide with Haman's story in a big way.

King Xerxes threw a huge, lavish party that lasted for seven full days to show off his wealth and power. The king, thoroughly drunk, decided to show off his beautiful queen. He summoned for her to come dressed in her royal robe. Queen Vashti refused. This greatly embarrassed the king. He burned with anger. He put out a formal decree that Vashti be stripped of her status as queen and never enter his presence again.

It was time to find a new queen. All the young and beautiful women of the kingdom were brought to the palace one by one to spend the evening with the king. Sort of an ancient *Bachelor* TV show.

The young woman selected was Esther, the orphaned Hebrew girl raised by Mordecai. That's right, Mordecai, the same man that Haman had it in for. No one made the connection because Esther kept her nationality concealed.

Esther was crowned as queen. But her people were soon to be destroyed. Time was running out. Mordecai sent word to his niece and told her that she must go before the king and plead for mercy for her people before it was too late.

She reminded her uncle Mordecai that a queen cannot just go into the presence of the king. She must be summoned. A queen could lose her life and certainly her position for messing with this rule.

Mordecai responded with a declaration that is worthy of a Hollywood film: He said:

"Do not think that because you are _____, you alone of all the Jews will escape. For if you remain silent at this time, _____ for the Jews will arise from another place, but you and your father's family _____. And who knows but that you have come to your royal position for _____?" (Esther 4:13–14 NIV)

The same is true for us. God's ultimate victory is certain. Is this not the promise of Romans 8:28?

In all things _____ works for the good of those who _____ (NIV).

There will be decrees and bullies along the way. But God will triumph. There will be dark times and battles. The question is not will He win, but will we suit up for His team.

Esther made her choice.

"I will go to _____, even though it is against the law. And if I _____, I perish" (Esther 4:16 NIV).

Since the rule of the king was audience by invitation only, there was only one hope for someone who dared to enter without being invited. The king had to stretch out his gold scepter in favor of the visit. One queen had already been dismissed. Esther could be next. For three days Esther prayed for favor, and then entered the throne room without being summoned. Maybe Xerxes was in a good mood, maybe he was allured by her beauty, maybe he genuinely loved Esther. Whatever the reason, he not only welcomed her with outstretched scepter, he told her to ask for whatever she wanted, up to half the kingdom.

Esther requested a small dinner party with the king and Haman. The king agreed and it took place that very evening.

Haman went home with a swagger. Feeling massive momentum, Haman decided to erect a seventy-five-foot-high pole, with the intention of securing the king's permission to impale Mordecai on it. So, the pole went up with full anticipation.

It just so happened that the king had trouble sleeping that night. He had no sheep to count or NyQuil to take, so he had a servant read him a book that contained a daily log of all that had happened under his reign —the Chronicles of Xerxes. In the reading they *just so happened* to come across an entry that spoke of a time when none other than Mordecai blew the whistle on two villains in the king's court who were plotting his assassination. Xerxes inquired as to whether or not he had done anything to honor Mordecai for this heroic act. He hadn't.

The next morning when Haman arrived at the palace to make his request, the king asked him a question. "What should the king do to honor someone who has brought great delight to the king?" Arrogant Haman assumed the king was referring to him, so he suggested that this person be put in royal robes and led through the city streets and praised.

The king said, "Good idea! I want you to go fetch Mordecai, put the robe on him, and I want you to personally drive him through town in my stretch limo."

Can you imagine the sick feeling in Haman's stomach? Haman left the palace to perform this hideous assignment. This did not seem to be the best time to get permission to impale Mordecai on the seventy-five-foot pole.

After the private parade of one, it was time for dinner with the king. At the meal, Esther made her request that her people, the Israelites, be saved from coming extermination. This was the first time she revealed her nationality to anyone. The king inquired about who would order such an attack against his queen and her people, and Esther said, "You are sitting next to him; it is Haman!"

The king decided to impale Haman on the very pole that had been prepared for Mordecai.

Mordecai was given Haman's position and his estate.

Mordecai's first order of business was the irreversible edict that Haman set in motion to execute all the Jews. He secured the king's blessing to send out another edict that would allow the Jews to defend themselves. It was the best he could do.

Non-Jewish people all over the 127 provinces of the Persian Empire attacked individual Jewish families in the greedy hope of looting their possessions. The Israelites were ready and over the next few days they defeated 75,800 people! In the midst of a dark and shaky time, God used Esther to turn it around.

Are you facing a situation right now that seems dark? Complicated? Hopeless?

Take a tip from Mordecai and Esther, and put your hope in this promise: God will ultimately win.

In all things God works for the good of those who love him... (Romans 8:28 NIV).

Because of that promise, we can make this our own: I will do what is right and trust God for the outcome.

QUESTIONS FOR REFLECTION:

1. When God says He will work all things for good for those who love Him, does that mean things will go the way we want?

_____

_____

_____

_____

2. God's responsibility is to see that all things work together for good. What is our responsibility? How do we live that out daily?

_____

_____

_____

_____

3. How might God be using you as an "Esther" to help others?

_____

_____

_____

_____

_____

Praying the Promise:

Father God, You give me unshakable hope through every season.
No matter what I walk through, I can be confident
that You are working it together for good.
Help me to keep my heart soft toward You no matter the circumstances.
Let my actions be just and right in Your eyes.
I trust You with my future,
because I know Your plans for me are good.
Amen.

CHAPTER FIFTEEN:

YOUR BEST DAYS ARE AHEAD

Several years ago when our children were small, we traveled to New York City to see the Macy's Thanksgiving Day Parade. We arrived on Tuesday, which may have been a mistake. A full day on Wednesday shopping and sightseeing left us so tired that we overslept on Thursday morning.

I awoke about the time the parade was passing down a nearby avenue. The girls were sound asleep. Knowing there was no hope of getting them ready, I determined to video the sights. I ran down the street only to find the signs of a parade already past: soda cups on the sidewalk, streamers on the street, sweepers cleaning up the mess.

I looked down the parade path and saw the backside of the disappearing celebration—a high floating image of Bullwinkle. I sighed and thought: "All this effort and all I get is a picture of Bullwinkle's inflated bottom."

Maybe you feel the same. You think the parade has passed you by. And perhaps all you can see right now is something that looks more like the bottom than the top of what life has to offer. But I want you to understand something. Even in these trying times when nothing seems to be going as you planned, God is at work. And He has not forgotten you.

Have you ever felt like your best days were behind you? From the business man who reminisces about his glory college days, to the girl who still laments about her first and lost high school sweetheart, it is easy to get stuck in yesterday. But I have a beautiful and trustworthy guarantee for you. Haggai 2:9 (NIV) promises:

The glory of this _____ will be greater than the _____.

Sometimes difficult circumstances are permitted in order for us to be sure we have not forgotten Him. Sometimes life has to come down to pig slop and whale guts for us to turn our attention back to God.

The prodigal son can tell you about the pig slop. He smelled it, felt it, and served it. He may have even tasted it. In one of Jesus' best-known stories, Jesus described the pigpen experience of a stubborn-hearted son. The boy, born in privilege, demanded his inheritance before his father's death. He took the money to a first-century equivalent of Monte Carlo. Within a few days, he was on a first-name basis with the casino manager. Within a few more, he was dead broke, looking for a job. He found one feeding pigs. The salary must have stunk as much as the swine did, because the boy was soon drooling over pig slop. He seriously considered taking a place at the trough and digging in.

It is probably in that moment when he came to his senses and got back on track with his life.

But, it took some pig slop to get his attention.

And it took whale guts to get Jonah's. Jonah had a problem with God's call on his life. God sent him to preach to the Ninevites and he did not want to. They could face the fire and smell the brimstone as far as he cared. Jonah was not about to help out a bunch of foreigners. God responded by putting Jonah in a time-out: three days in the bowel system of a big fish. The whale couldn't stomach Jonah any longer than that. Next thing Jonah knew he was on the beach, dripping of salt water and gastric juices. He got the point and got back on track.

The prodigal and the pigs. Jonah and the fish. They came face to face with some pretty low times. But they were not forgotten. Instead, they were being re-directed to something better.

So how does God get our attention when we fail to give Him ours?

According to a page out of His playbook: He might let us stink with pigs and sink with whales. You might go through a drought, a downturn, or a difficulty. We've all felt it—that chill in the corner office, a dent in the savings account, a lonely wind through the house. A sense of nagging futility that you just cannot shake. You plant much, but seem to harvest little. You eat, but never have enough. You drink but never have your fill. You dress, but never feel warm. You earn wages, only to see them disappear. Life does not work. Your finest endeavors collapse like sandcastles in a tsunami.

Let's be careful, here. We do not need to attribute every single setback or struggle to God's discipline. No need to get philosophical over each red light or headache. There are, however, seasons of God-ordained struggle, times of exhaustive emptiness. These days exist for one purpose: to turn our hearts back to God's house. When nothing quenches our deepest thirsts, when no achievements abate our restless hunger, when droughts turn our fields into deserts and retirements into pocket change, what can we do? God's answer is clear. Give careful thought to your ways. Evaluate your priorities. Assess your strategies.

Ask yourself: Is God's big thing my big thing? Are my purposes aligned with His?

For many of you the answer is a resounding "yes." His priority is your priority. His passion is your passion: you want God's presence to be felt in every building and borough of the world.

But many others would have to give a different answer. What is the equivalent of pig slop and whale guts you are experiencing? Chemical dependency? Selfish ambition? Empty days and lonely nights? The hollow pursuit of stuff?

Perhaps you started off with the right priorities. You gave your heart to God and your life to God's work. But then came the kids, the promotion, the transfer, the long hours, the business trips. With each passing day you thought less about God's work and more about yours. Tithing became tipping, prayers became rote quotes. You did not forget God, but you did not remember Him either. Life just does not work like you hoped.

And now God has pulled you aside for a face-to-face. It is time to consider your ways. It is time to wash off the pig slop, to shower off the fish guts, and recognize that you were made for so much more. God wants you to move in step with Him, so you can rejoice in His riches and find peace, joy, and contentment when your heart beats in sync with His.

Greater things are ahead for those who turn their hearts toward Him.

This is one case where the war is won through the act of surrender. So if you are feeling a bit shaky and tired of the turmoil you are in, prayerfully consider if a change in course might be exactly where God is leading you— out of the darkness and into His light.

In God's plan, the future is always brighter, the next chapter is always sweeter, and tomorrow always has the potential to outshine today. That is good news for people in the pigpens and whales' bellies of life. To the person who feels like the best days have come and gone, God offers this hope-drenched promise from Haggai 2:9 (NIV):

The _____ of this present house will be _____ than the former house.

GOD'S PROMISE:

The latter will be better than the former!

MY PROMISE:

I will make God's work my work.

Let's face it. Most of us do not like to have our flaws pointed out to us. Then to have someone lead off the nagging lecture with the words, "The Lord says..." Well, chances are good the message will be tuned out. And maybe even the messenger turned out.

Nobody likes to be the bearer of bad news. But when God tells you to say something, you just might find yourself having to choose between pleasing the Lord or pleasing man. You cannot serve two masters. Such was the plight of Haggai. And fortunately for the Hebrews, Haggai chose well and delivered God's message. It was for their own good, really. Sometimes medicine can be hard to swallow, but it is exactly what is needed. To understand the situation, you first need a little background.

The children of Israel had passed the last seventy winters in Babylonian exile. Their city was razed and beloved Temple was ransacked. But, after seven decades, a tunnel of sunlight pierced the clouds and surprised the people.

In the first year of King Cyrus' reign in Persia, the Lord moved on the heart of the king to make a proclamation throughout his realm, and also to put it in writing that they were to build a temple for Him.

God turned the heart of King Cyrus toward the Jews and turned the Jews toward Jerusalem. In 538 BC a delegation of fifty thousand Jews, prompted by God and funded by Cyrus, made the nine-hundred-mile trek back to Jerusalem. They rolled up the sleeves of their robes and got to work. Initially, God's big thing was their big thing.

Dissenters and outsiders tried first to infiltrate, and later to discourage the Temple builders. But the Jews maintained their resolve. They stayed focused on God's big thing. They made God's priority their priority. After a few years, however, they began to grow weary. Perhaps the stone-stacking was too tiresome, or the criticism too irksome. Or maybe they began thinking of their own projects; their farms, houses, and businesses. One by one, little by little, person by person, they turned away from God's big thing and quit working on the Temple. God's big thing became their small thing.

And, before they knew it, sixteen years came and went. Sixteen years! Enough time for grass to grow and cover the footers of the foundation. Enough time for neighboring nations to conclude that Israel's God was not worth any devotion. Enough time for a generation of Jewish children to look at the abandoned temple like a forgotten construction project.

Meanwhile, as God's house languished, the houses of the Jews flourished. Sort of. While the former exiles built businesses, enterprises and fine panel houses, to their surprise they grew more and more miserable by the day. Something needed to change. At least, that was the message that poor Haggai was charged with delivering. The prophet asked them how it was that they had time to build their own houses but not God's temple? Then came the hard dose of reality. He said, "You have planted much, but have harvested little. You eat, but never have enough. You drink, but never have your fill. You put on clothes but are not warm. You earn wages, only to put them in a purse with holes in it." (See Haggai 1:4–11.)

Despite their best efforts to make themselves fat and happy, they were actually neither. They had grown so focused on themselves that they were neglecting what God called them to do. So he reminded them of their initial calling. Go up the mountain. Bring down the timber. Build the house. Honor the Lord with your effort. According to the words of Haggai, God made their selfish efforts fruitless in order to get their attention.

Want to know how God responds to lethargy and misplaced priorities? You just heard it. Ever wondered what God does when we make His big thing a small thing and our small things big things? Now you know.

God told them, through Haggai, to take action. Perhaps it is time to consider your ways. Military folks have a great term for this—an about-face. The soldier who marches south, pivots, and marches north. The infantry who marches west, pivots, and steps east. About-face. One-hundred-eighty-degree turn. Change of direction. Change of intention. Change of heart. Repentance. Ahhh, there is the religious word. Repent. Turn. Re-direct yourself.

Amazingly, the Jews did.

The Lord stirred up the leadership and the people got to work on the house of God. Haggai's message was both delivered and received. And God blessed their renewed spirit. Twice He assured them, "I am with you."

And He is with you. It is not too late to start again. To a congregation full of saints, God said:

"I have this against you, that you have left your first love. _____ therefore from where you have fallen; _____ and _____" (Revelation 2:4–5 NKJV).

Three steps:

• Remember.

- Repent.

- Do the first works.

Remember God's high call on your life. He led you out of Babylon and into your homeland.

Repent from misplaced priorities.

"Seek first the _____ and his righteousness, and _____ shall be added to you" (Matthew 6:33 NIV).

Do the first works. What are these, you ask? Prayer. Worship. Service. Study. The basics.

Start there.

God keeps His promises. Make His work your work, and the latter will be greater than the former.

God's great promise:

"The glory of this present house will be _____ than the glory of the former house," says the LORD **Almighty. "And in this place I will _____"** (Haggai 2:9 NIV).

The glory of the latter temple will be greater than the former. Or, in your case, the glory of the latter career, the latter years, the latter attempts, the latter days of marriage, the latter seasons of life will be greater than the former.

With God, the best is always yet to be. It simply falls on each of us to heed the words that Haggai implored to the Jews and make our own promise.

My promise: "I will make God's work my work."

QUESTIONS FOR REFLECTION:

1. What are moments in your life when you have felt a part of God's work? How has He used you?

_____

_____

_____

_____

_____

2. Where do you see God working right now?

_____

_____

_____

_____

_____

3. What are some practical ways you can make God's work your work?

_____

_____

_____

_____

_____

_____

Praying the Promise:

Father, I am so grateful that You have called me to be a co-laborer with You.
I believe You can take me as I am today
and use me for Your work and Your glory.
I set my heart on You, Lord.
As I seek first Your kingdom,
I trust that You are adding to my life everything I need
to accomplish Your plans.
I believe my best days are ahead.
Amen.

CHAPTER SIXTEEN:

GOD'S GOOD IS FOR OUR GOOD

In the spring of 2010, a skiing accident took the life of Tara Storch's thirteen-year-old daughter, Taylor. What followed for Tara and her husband, Todd, was every parent's worst nightmare: a funeral, a burial, a flood of questions and tears. They decided to donate their daughter's organs to needy patients. Meanwhile, few people needed a heart more than Patricia Winters. Her heart had begun to fail five years earlier, leaving her too weak to do much more than sleep. Taylor's heart gave Patricia a fresh start on life.

Tara had only one request: she wanted to hear the heart of her daughter. She and her husband flew from Dallas to Phoenix and went to the home of Patricia. The two embraced for a long time, soon to be joined by Todd. After a few moments, Tara took a stethoscope and placed it against Patricia's chest and heard her daughter's heartbeat again:

"It is so strong," the mother whispered.

"She is very strong," Patricia assured.

Mom and Dad took turns listening to Taylor's heart. Even though it dwells in a different body, they heard the still-beating heart of their daughter. And, when God hears your heart, He hears the still-beating heart of His Son. As Paul said:

It is no longer _____, but Christ _____ (Galatians 2:20 NKJV).

The apostle sensed within himself, not just the philosophy, ideals, or influence of Christ, but the person of Jesus. Christ moved in. He still does. When grace happens, Christ enters.

Christ _____, the _____ of glory (Colossians 1:27 NKJV).

For many years, I missed this truth. I believed all of the other prepositions: Christ for me, with me, ahead of me. And I knew I was working beside Christ, under Christ, with Christ. But I never imagined that Christ was *in* me.

I cannot blame my deficiency on Scripture. Paul refers to this union 216 times. John mentions it twenty-six. They describe a Christ who not only woos us to Himself, but "ones" us to Himself. First John 4:13 (NIV) says:

Whoever _____ that Jesus is the Son of God, God _____ and he in God.

No other religion or philosophy makes such a claim. No other movement implies the living presence of its founder in his followers. Mohammed does not indwell Muslims. Buddha does not inhabit Hindus. Hugh Hefner does not inhabit the pleasure-seeking hedonist. Influence? Instruct? Entice? Yes. But occupy? No.

Yet, Christians embrace this inscrutable promise. Colossians 1:27 (MSG) says:

The mystery in a nutshell is this: _____.

The Christian is a person in whom Christ is happening.

We are Jesus Christ's; we belong to Him. But even more, we are increasingly Him. He moves in and commandeers our hands and feet; requisitions our minds and tongues. We sense His rearranging: debris into divine, pig's ear into silk purses. He repurposes bad decisions and squalored choices. Little by little an image emerges.

Romans 8:29 (NIV) says:

He decided at the outset to _____ of those who love him along the same lines as his Son.

God's plan for you is nothing short of a new heart. If you were a car, God would want control of your engine. If you were a computer, God would claim the software and the hard drive. If you were an airplane, He would take His seat in the cockpit. But you are a person, so God wants to change your heart.

But you were taught to be _____, to become a new person. That new person is made to be like God—made to be _____ (Ephesians 4:23–24 NIV).

Is that not good news? You are not stuck with today's personality. You are not condemned to "grumpydom." You are tweakable. Even if you have worried each day of your life, you needn't worry the rest of your life. So what if you were born a bigot? You do not have to die one.

Where did we get the idea we cannot change? From whence come statements such as, "It is just my nature to worry," or, "I will always be pessimistic. I am just that way," or, "I have a bad temper. I cannot help the way I react"?

Says who?

Would we make similar statements about our bodies? "It is just my nature to have a broken leg. I cannot do anything about it." Of course not. If our bodies malfunction, we seek help. Shouldn't we do the same with our hearts? Shouldn't we seek aid for our sour attitudes? Can we not request treatment for our selfish tirades? Of course we can. Jesus can change our hearts. He wants us to have a heart like His.

Can you imagine a better offer?

Philippians 2:13 is a promise He makes to you and me:

It is _____ who works in you both _____

according to his good purpose (NIV).

God is eager to help you experience new strength and new hope as you allow Him to live out through you.

GOD'S PROMISE:

I will work in and through you.

MY PROMISE:

I welcome and cooperate with the inner work of God.

When we think of Mary, the mother of Jesus, we think of Christmas stories. We think of Bethlehem, the manger and the baby Jesus. It is right to do so. Yet, I wonder if the story of Mary is more than a story of Christ's first coming. Might it, might she, be a picture of what Christ wants to do in us?

Mary, in a moment of disclosure, related what the angel Gabriel said to her.

"The _____ will come on you, and the power of _____ will overshadow you. So the holy one to be born will be called the Son of God" (Luke 1:35 NIV).

The essence of God was reduced to the size of a freckle, enwombed in the recesses of Mary, where he grew, expanded, and kicked until the miracle of gestation became the moment of delivery. And the voice of God filled the Bethlehem sky.

Mary heard the baby cry. She heard Him because she was willing to believe the wildest of promises. Can we call it the promise of regeneration? Cumbersome word, for sure, but it is used by theologians to describe this miracle, first seen in Mary—then offered to any who would follow in her steps. The Mary Miracle is Christ in you.

Yes, you and me. We are Marys in the making! Embedded in Philippians 2:13 is this astounding truth:

It is God who works _____ both to will and to act according to his good purpose (Philippians 2:13 NIV).

God is working in you! He is at work to help you want to do and be able to do what pleases Him. He will change your "want to" to "can do." Ezekiel 36:26–28 says it this way:

"I will give you a _____ and put a _____ in you; I will remove from you your heart of _____ and give you a heart of _____. And I will put my Spirit in you and move you to follow my decrees and be careful to keep my laws. Then you will live in the land I gave your ancestors; you will be _____, and I will be _____."

Who is the active party described in this passage? Who does the work? Who takes the people and gathers them together? Who cleanses and deposits a new spirit? Who removes the heart of stone—cold and hard—and implants the heart of flesh—pliable and life giving? Who gives the Spirit and the desire to obey divine decrees?

The answers?

God.

God.

God.

God.

God.

God.

Ephesians 2:5 tells us it is God who:

...made us _____ with Christ even when we were _____ in transgressions—it is by _____ you have been saved (NIV).

And in the words of John 1:12–13 (NIV), it is God who gave us:

...the right to become _____— children born not of natural descent, nor of human decision or a husband's will, but _____.

All this is from God! He calls us to Himself and gives us a new life. Every part of us is affected by this regeneration: our guilt is washed, our future is bright, and our wisdom and strength is heaven-sent. This is what it means to be "born again."

God gives you the same offer He gave Mary—the supernatural deposit of His son in your life. Scripture is replete with the promise: Jesus lives in his children. Paul's prayer for the Ephesians was:

That Christ may _____ through faith (Ephesians 3:17 NIV).

What is the mystery of the gospel?

Christ _____, the hope of glory (Colossians 1:27 NIV).

John was clear:

Those who obey his commands live _____ and he _____ (I John 3:24 NIV).

And the sweetest invitation from Christ in Revelation 3:20:

"Here I am! I stand at the door and knock. If anyone hears my voice and opens the door, I will _____ and eat _____ and he _____" (NKJV).

Take note of the precious preposition—"in." Christ is not just near you or for you or with you—He is longing to be in you. God offers you the same Christmas gift He gave Mary—the indwelling Christ. Christ grew in her until He came out. Christ will grow in you until the same occurs. Christ will come out in your speech, in your actions, in your decisions. Every place you live will be a Bethlehem, and every day you live will be a Christmas. You, like Mary, will deliver Christ into the world.

He was an embryo in her. He is a force in you. And if we'll listen, He'll direct our actions.

I sensed His corrective pull recently at a Sunday service. A dear woman stopped me as I was entering the church building. She did not agree with a comment I made in a sermon the week before and wanted to express her opinion...in the foyer...in a loud voice...ten minutes prior to the service. What is more, she pressed the nerve of my pet peeve. "Other people feel the same way." Grrr. Who are these "other people"? How many "other people" are there? And why, for crying out loud, do not "other people" come and talk to me?

By now it was time for the service to begin. And now I was in more of a mood to hunt bear than preach. I couldn't get my mind off the woman and the "other people." I drove home from the morning assembly beneath a cloud. Rather than love, joy, peace, and patience, I felt anger, frustration, and impatience. I was completely out of step with the Spirit. And I had a choice. I could march to my own beat, or I could get back in rhythm. I knew what to do.

I made the phone call and told her, "I did not feel like we quite finished the conversation we began in the foyer." So we did. And over the next fifteen minutes we discovered that our differences were based on a misunderstanding and "the other people" consisted of her and her husband and he was really okay.

Peace was restored when I got back in step with the rhythm of His heartbeat. To walk in the Spirit, respond to the promptings God gives you. Learn to wait, to be silent, to listen for His voice. Cherish stillness, sensitize yourself to His touch.

Just think—you do not need a thing! All God's gifts are right in front of you as you wait expectantly for Jesus to arrive on the scene (1 Corinthians 1:7–8 MSG). You needn't hurry or scurry. The Spirit-led life does not panic, it trusts.

Mary had plenty of reason to resist, doubt, and fear. But she trusted the words of an angel and carried the hope of the world within her. That same hope indwells you.

And that same hand that also pushed the rock from the tomb can shove away your doubt. The same power that stirred the still heart of Christ can stir your flagging faith. The same strength that put Satan on his heels can, and will, defeat Satan in your life. The same power that brought Christ into Mary's world will bring Christ into yours. He is working within us, so that, like Mary, we can become vessels for the greatest gift of all. Jesus Christ.

This is His promise. Let's, together, agree with and declare this promise.

My promise: "I will welcome and cooperate with the inner work of God."

QUESTIONS FOR REFLECTION:

1. What does it mean to you to have a "heart of flesh"?

_____

_____

_____

_____

_____

2. What kind of work do you sense God doing inside of you? How can you cooperate with His Holy Spirit?

_____

_____

_____

_____

_____

3. If Jesus truly lives in your inner person, how should your outward person look and act?

_____

_____

_____

_____

_____

_____

Praying the Promise:

Jesus, I believe You dwell in my inner person.
You have given me a brand-new heart,
and You have filled me with Your love and power.
I desire to walk in perfect step with Your plans and purposes.
Help my faith to increase that I may allow You
to live through me from the inside out.
Amen.

CHAPTER SEVENTEEN:

JESUS UNDERSTANDS

I once waded into the Jordan River. On a trip to Israel, my family and I stopped to see the traditional spot of Jesus' baptism. It is a charming place. Sycamores cast their shadows. Birds chirp. The water invites. So I accepted the invitation and waded in to be baptized.

No one wanted to join me, so I immersed myself in the water. I declared my belief in Christ and sank so low into the river I could touch the bottom. When I did, I felt a stick and pulled it out. Well, what do you know—a baptism memento? Some people get certificates or Bibles; I got a stick. I keep it on my office credenza, so I can show it to fear-filled people.

When they chronicle their anxieties about the economy or concern about their kids, I hand them the stick. I tell them how God muddied His feet on our world of diapers, death, digestion, and disease. How John told him to stay on the riverbank, but Jesus wouldn't listen. How He came to earth for this very purpose, to become one of us. "Why, He might have touched this very stick," I like to say. As they smile, I ask, "Since He came this far to reach us, cannot we take our fears to Him?"

Maybe this has been your own question. Does God have time for my problems?

My sick child.

My loan payment.

The layoffs at work.

The broken heater.

In the vastness of the universe, with all the big-picture items He has on His plate, does He really care about those things?

Jesus understands us because He became one of us. Had He become a light, a force, a heavenly voice or image, we would have been amazed, but He became flesh. He took on the form of a human being. He was, at once, fully human and fully divine. John 1:14 (NIV) puts it this way:

The Word became _____ and made his dwelling among us. We have seen his glory, the glory of the one and only Son, who came _____, full of grace and truth.

Had God become a human without birth—certainly possible for God, who made Adam out of dust—we would admire Him, but never draw near to Him. After all, how could a God who descended to earth comprehend earthly life? Had God been biologically conceived with two earthly parents —certainly possible for a God who created you and me by two parents—we would draw near to Him, but would we want to worship Him? After all, is He really different than you and me?

But if He was both, at once God and man, then we have the best of both worlds. Neither His humanity nor deity compromised. We draw near to Christ because He was fully human. We worship Christ because He was fully divine. He was like us, but more than us. And He navigated through this world so that He could show us the way.

Some years ago I served as the teacher at a week-long Bible retreat. There is much to recall about the event. The food was phenomenal. The seaside setting was spectacular. I made several new friends. Yet, of all the memories, the one I will never forget is the Friday night basketball game.

The idea was hatched the moment that David arrived. The attendees did not know he was coming, but the moment he walked into the room, they knew who he was: David Robinson.

NBA All-Star. MVP. Three-time Olympian. Two-time gold medal winner. Dream Team member.

Two-time NBA Champion. College All-American. By the end of the first day, someone asked me, "Any chance that he would play basketball with us?"

He was seven feet and one inch of raw talent. Body, ripped. Skills, honed. Basketball IQ, legendary. Us was a collection of pudgy, middle-aged, well-meaning but out of shape fellows. Bodies, plump. Skills, pathetic. Basketball IQ, slightly less than that of a squirrel. Still, I asked David. And David, in an utter display of indulgence, said yes.

We set the game, *the game*, on the schedule for the last night of the seminar, Friday night. Attendance in the seminar declined. Attendance on the basketball court increased. Fellows who hadn't dribbled a ball since middle school could be seen heaving shot after shot at the basket. The net was seldom threatened.

The night of the game, *the game*, David walked onto the court for the first time all week. As he warmed up, the rest of us stopped. The ball fit in his hand like a tennis ball would in mine. He carried on conversations while dribbling the ball, spinning the ball on a finger, and passing the ball behind his back. When the game began, it was David and we children. We all knew he was holding back. Still, he took two strides for our one. He caught the ball with one hand instead of two. When he passed the ball, it was more a missile than a pass. He played basketball at a level we could only dream about.

At one point, just for the fun of it, I suppose, he let loose. The same guy who had slam-dunked basketballs over the likes of Michael Jordan and Charles Barkley let it go. I suppose he just couldn't hold it back any longer. With three strides he went from half court to rim. The pudgy middle-aged opposition cleared a path as he sailed, head level with the basket, and slammed the ball with a force that left the backboard shaking.

We gulped.

David smiled.

We got the message. *That's how the game is meant to be played.*

Jesus got in the game so that He could show us how it was meant to be played. Hebrews 4:15–16 (NIV) says:

For our high priest [Jesus] is able to _____ our weaknesses. When he lived on earth he was tempted in every way that we are, but he did not sin. Let us, then, feel very sure that we can _____ _____ where there is grace. There we can receive mercy and grace to _____ when we need it.

GOD'S PROMISE:

I know your sufferings and weaknesses.

> ## MY PROMISE:
>
> *I will draw near to God with confidence that He hears and understands me.*

"The Word became flesh and dwelt among us." That's how John 1:14 describes it. The Living Word that brought light to the void of darkness, and spun the earth into orbit, now here with creation, speaking peace to the storms, hope to the broken, and life to the dead.

The Son of God came in a humble way. Not as many assumed He would come as royalty, positioned to step into His place of authority. No, His path was dustier, His hands more calloused, His journey more common. For He walked the path not just of a King, but of a kid. Jesus was, at once, fully human and fully divine. He was the Son of God, but He came to us born of a woman. He was like other babies.

First breath.

First cry.

First steps.

His first few days were spent in a feeding-trough. (Not exactly the room-with-a-view you would expect the King of heaven to get.) But the animals made room, the hay was warm, and the Savior had come. The world received a miracle in a manger.

His childhood was a normal one. His earthly father a carpenter. Sitting by his side, watching him drive the nails through the wood, turn something jagged into something beautiful. Gathering firewood for His mother. Eating with His siblings. Going to the synagogue for lessons. The simple things that make up a childhood, a life.

Luke 2:52 tells us:

Jesus grew in _____ and _____, and in _____ with God and man (NIV).

His body developed. His muscles grew. His bones matured. There is no evidence or suggestion that He was spared the inconveniences of adolescence. He may have been gangly or homely. He knew the pain of sore muscles or the sting of salt in an open wound.

He was weary enough to sit down at a well and sleepy enough to doze off in a rocking boat. He became hungry in the wilderness and thirsty on the cross. When the soldiers pounded the nail through His skin, a thousand nerve endings cried for relief. As He hung limp on the cross, two human lungs begged for oxygen.

The Word became flesh. Supreme divinity found fully in humanity. Such is the message of Colossians 1:15–20 (NIV):

The Son is the _____ of the invisible God, the firstborn over all creation. For in him all things were created: things in heaven and on earth, visible and invisible, whether thrones or powers or rulers or authorities; all things have been created _____ him and _____ him. He is before all things, and _____ all things hold together. And he is the head of the body, the church; he is the _____ and the firstborn from among the dead, so that in everything he might have the supremacy. For God was pleased to have _____ dwell in him,

and through him to reconcile to himself all things, whether things on earth or things in heaven, by making _____ through his_____, shed on the cross.

This is what characterized the first-century church. Those who had lived close enough to touch Him came to this stunning conclusion: He is the image of the invisible God.

You thought the moon affects the tides? It does. But Christ runs the moon.

You thought the United States is a super power? The United States only has the power Christ gives, and nothing more. He has authority over everything. And He has had it forever.

Yet, in spite of this lofty position, He was willing, for a time, to forgo privileges of divinity and, without measure, enter humanity. But not one drop of divinity was lost in the change to humanity. He was fully human AND fully God, what theologians call the hypostatic union. The fullness of God, every bit of Him, took residence in the body of Christ. The star maker, for a time, built cabinets in Nazareth.

Does this miracle of incarnation matter? This idea that the Son of God came to us as a baby in a manger and walked this earth as a man? It does if you are bedridden. It does if you battle disease. It does if chronic pain is a part of your life. The One who hears your prayers understands your pain.

What hope this gives us! Nothing is beneath Him. Nothing is too common, too small, or too insignificant for His attention or aid. He understands. He never shrugs or scoffs or dismisses physical struggle.

He Himself had a human body, and He understands.

Does this miracle matter? If you ever wonder if God understands you, it does. If you ever wonder if God listens, it does. If you ever wonder if the Uncreated Creator can, in a million years, comprehend the life of a truck driver, housewife, or immigrant, then ponder long and hard this promise. God says: "I understand you and I always will."

Are you troubled in spirit? Scripture tells us He was, too.

Are you so anxious that you could die? He was, too.

Are you overwhelmed with grief? He was, too.

Do you ever need to find a place of peace and quiet? He did too.

Have you ever prayed with loud cries and tears? He did, too.

He gets you.

Because Jesus is human, He understands you. Because He is divine He can help you. But not if you do not go to Him. He did not remain aloof, so why would we? He did not keep His distance, so why would we keep ours?

This is God's promise to us: **"Our high priest is able to understand our weaknesses."** Therefore this can be our promise to Him:

I will draw near to God with confidence that He hears and understands me.

QUESTIONS FOR REFLECTION:

1. Why is it important to understand that Jesus was both fully human and fully God?

_____

_____

_____

_____

_____

2. Jesus experienced everything we will ever experience, except for one thing. What is that one thing?

_____

_____

_____

_____

3. What does it mean to you in a practical sense to know Jesus suffered pain? How does His suffering help you in your suffering?

_____

_____

_____

_____

_____

PRAYING THE PROMISE:

Jesus, You suffered in all the ways I ever will and more,
yet You did not sin.
You humbled yourself,
so you could take on the weight of my sin.
You left your heavenly Father,
so I could know He will never leave or forsake me.
You hear my prayers. You know my pain.
You bring me peace.
When I face trouble, I take heart,
for I know that You have overcome the world.

CHAPTER EIGHTEEN:

ALL THINGS FOR THOSE WHO SEEK GOD

When explorers from Europe began to discover the South Pacific Islands, they encountered people who knew nothing of the outside world. Their entire world consisted of their island. They measured wealth in seashells and believed the sky was a canopy supported by trees. They'd never struck a match, heard the roar of an engine, been told about gravity, or experienced a cold day. As far as they knew, all of humanity consisted of what they could see: tanned tribesmen who indwelt the jagged valleys and the misty plateaus of New Guinea.

We can forgive the Highlanders if they weren't always hospitable. They'd never seen skin so white, faces so hairy, bodies so clothed, or behavior so bizarre. They'd never seen soap lather (they thought it was a disease) or lantern light (they thought the explorers owned a piece of the moon).

They honestly thought the universe consisted of *their* island. When the explorers told them otherwise, the natives did not know what to think.

Since the beginning of time, man has tried to build his own kingdoms in the sky: from the pyramids of Egypt to the empires of Rome to the skyscrapers on Wall Street. In displays of conquest and acquisition from the battlefield to the boardroom, many have worked with all their might to build a powerful kingdom. But history tells us that every kingdom on this earth has proven to be collapsible. Kings fall, dominions are destroyed, powers are displaced, and presidents are removed.

But do not think for a moment that kingdoms are only built by the mighty in power. No, the truth is, we are all tempted to build our own little kingdoms. Tempted to self-promote, rank ourselves on the totem pole of success, and become pridefully consumed in the achievements of our own lives. We become consumed with our own towers of accomplishment and power. And for all the things that man accomplishes in his pursuits, good or bad, it eventually comes to an end.

But what if there was a kingdom different than all of our worldly kingdoms? What if there was a kingdom that could not be toppled, conquered, or overthrown?

The prophets of the Old Testament envisioned a time when God would affirm and establish His rule in a new way: In Jeremiah 32, God said:

"They shall be _____, and I will be their God; then I will give them _____ and _____, that they may fear me forever, for the _____ of them and their children after them" (Jeremiah 32:38–39 NIV).

The prophets promised the arrival of an anointed King, a Messiah, one uniquely related to God to serve as the instrument of His rule:

Your _____ is coming to you; He is _____ and having _____, lowly and _____ (Zechariah 9:9 NKJV).

Notice it did not say that He would be exalted and riding in a chariot. No, in stark contrast from what would be expected, it said, "lowly and riding on a donkey." Not exactly what you would expect to hear about the ruler of a mighty kingdom. And many missed this. They were looking for a king like the kings of earth. And they expected a kingdom that would be established here on earth. But God's plans were much different and far bigger than the establishment of a physical empire.

Why? Because He knew that earthly establishments pass away. They are built on a shaky foundation. But He was establishing something that would not be toppled by man. A far better kingdom.

The kingdoms of the world offer limited external peace. The kingdom of God offers eternal inner peace.

The kingdoms of the world offer joy based on circumstances. The kingdom of God offers joy regardless of circumstance.

The kingdoms of the earth judge innocent until proven guilty. The kingdom of God judges innocent even when guilty.

The kingdoms of the earth were built on the blood, sweat, and tears of many men. The kingdom of God was built on the blood, sweat, and tears of one man.

When the true King stepped on the scene, paradigms shifted and plans unraveled. It was not what they expected in the natural, but they would soon discover it was so much better. God's plan always is.

When our own kingdoms are shaking and falling around us, we are given the promise of Matthew 6:33:

"But seek first his kingdom and his righteousness, and all these things will be given to you as well."

GOD'S PROMISE:

When you seek Me, you will find Me and have all that you need.

MY PROMISE:

I will seek God's kingdom.

Christ came like an outsider into a remote island, an invader of sorts, challenging His followers to re-draw their maps. He cracked open worldviews and pressed people to come to terms with a different dimension, a grand commonwealth, a larger world, a kingdom.

The prophets promised the arrival of an anointed King, a Messiah, one uniquely related to God to serve as the instrument of his rule.

God-fearing Jews set their hope on the coming of the king. And, according to the New Testament, their hopes were realized in the form of a Nazarene carpenter whose handshake with the world included this phrase:

"The time has come. The _____ has come near. Repent and believe the good news!" (Mark 1:15 NIV)

With these words, Jesus not only began His ministry, He introduced His favorite subject: the kingdom of God. The term "kingdom of God" and its Jewish equivalent "kingdom of heaven" occur some sixty times in the first three Gospels. In the teachings of Jesus, the subject of a kingdom commands center stage.

The disciples expected Jesus to overthrow the Roman rule and establish His own kingdom on earth. But Jesus refused. In Acts 1:6, they gathered around Him and asked, "Lord, are You now going to restore the kingdom to Israel?" Jesus answered them, that an earthly kingdom was not their concern. And instead commissioned them to go into all the world to preach the good news of a heavenly kingdom.

We must tune our own ears and hearts to the answer that Jesus gave His anxious kingdom-craving disciples. Success and accomplishments here on earth are wonderful things. But Jesus was reminding them that the most important thing was the kingdom of God. In Matthew, Jesus told those who came to hear Him speak:

"Seek first the kingdom of God and his righteousness."

God's agenda culminates in a kingdom. And, according to Jesus, God's kingdom is less about boundaries and castles and more about changing hearts and minds.

In Mark 4, Jesus teaches them about the kingdom through a story:

"A farmer went out to sow his seed. As he was scattering the seed, some fell along the path, and the birds came and ate it up. Some fell on rocky places, where it did not have much soil. It sprang up quickly, because the soil was shallow. But when the sun came up, the plants were scorched, and they withered because they had no root. Other seed fell among thorns, which grew up and choked the plants, so that they did

not bear grain. Still other seed fell on _____. It came up, grew and produced a crop, some multiplying thirty, some sixty, some a hundred times" (Mark 4:3–9 NIV).

This kingdom enters—not like a nation with armies and weapons—but like a farmer with seed. The kingdom lands on hearts like a kernel on soil. If the heart is open the kingdom takes root. But if the heart is hard, the seed falls away. Most hearts are hard. According to Jesus' math, three out of four people resist the kingdom. But to those who open their hearts, Jesus gives a gift— entrance into a kingdom; an invisible kingdom of the "here and now" and a visible kingdom of the future.

Jesus announced, "The kingdom of God is in your midst." The Greek word translated "in the midst" means "within your reach." "Reach for it!" is the implied invitation. Those who do will discover a kingdom of great joy.

The kingdom is the treasure in a hidden field, the pearl of great value (see Matthew 13:44–46). Finding the kingdom is like finding a winning lottery ticket in the sock drawer or a discarded jewel worth a king's ransom. It is like finding out that this tiny island of life is but a dot in God's Pacific Ocean. It is the good news that we are not sentenced to life without parole on this cramped piece of dirt, but we are part of a kingdom, a kingdom where justice flows and peace settles like mist on the meadows of life. According to Jesus, only one thing matters, the kingdom of God.

This kingdom is worth everything you have, Jesus says. But to receive this kingdom, you have to trust a different voice than your own. Hear an authority higher than yourself. Indeed the highest prayer is this: "Our Father in heaven, hallowed be your name, your kingdom come" (Matthew 6:9–10). The kingdom is everything. And, it just so happens that our Father is King of the kingdom! If your father is the king, everything changes.

I always thought it would be great to meet a prince, to know the child of royalty. I would ask him some questions: Do you ever see the king in pajamas? Does he let you sit on his lap on the throne? I often wished I knew a royal family.

Then I remembered that I did. My hometown knew nothing of crowns and castles. But we were all about football. Every Friday night our small town would gather in the stadium sanctuary to lift holy praise to the mighty Mustangs. We worshiped football. And, since football was king, the head coach was, well, he was "King Leach."

He presided over all the freshmen players like a marine over his raw recruits. When he shouted "Jump!" we created a grasshopper chorus line. He was the high coach and we were his subjects. But my buddy Jim was his son.

I have a memory of the two of them, coach and son, leaving practice together: laughing, tossing a ball as they walked, headed toward the same dinner table. Jim had the coach for a dad. You and I have immeasurably more—we have the King of kings as ours. His Highness is our Father. The implications of this stagger us. He listens when we call. He cares when we fall. He includes us at His table and writes our name in His will.

If the king is an unknown fearless force who rules from the opposite side of a castle wall, you have a king and nothing more. But if the king is the man who butters your bread and tucks you in, and locks the door at night, you have more than a king; you have a reason to smile. You know the king's heart and the king knows your name and extends this unspeakable invitation: "Come and enter the kingdom of God."

Our King loves us, but we must be quick to add, His kingdom is not about us. We think it is, we assume it is. After all, are we not children of the king? The kingdom exists to make us happy, to fill us, to fulfill us, to fix us. The kingdom is about us, right?

No—it is about God. We get in on it, to be sure. We benefit, no doubt. But we are not the subject. God is. We are not the story—His kingdom is.

And His kingdom has one condition. And this condition is a deal-breaker. The kingdom has one king. The throne permits one occupant and that occupant is not moving. The role of "Your Highness" has been assigned to someone else. You and I are welcome to enter the throne room, but we have to surrender our crowns at the door, an act that, according to Jesus' math, 75 percent of the people are not willing to do. But for those who do, the benefits of the kingdom belong to them.

God's promise to us is that if we will seek first His kingdom and His righteousness, then all the other things will be given to us as well. In response to that promise, let's make this unshakable, immovable decision ourselves, saying:

I will seek first God's kingdom.

QUESTIONS FOR REFLECTION:

1. Think about the word "seek." What does it imply to you?

_____

_____

_____

_____

_____

2. How do you think you can seek something that you cannot see?

_____

_____

_____

_____

_____

3. What are "all these things" that you desire for God to add to you?

_____

_____

_____

_____

_____

_____

PRAYING THE PROMISE:

Jesus, You tell me to seek first Your kingdom.
Give me eyes to see the signs of Your kingdom in my everyday life.
Flood my imagination with Your vision for my family,
my church, my city, and this world.
Let my heart know and understand what You are doing in heaven
that I might be about your business here on earth.
In Your name, I pray.
Amen.

CHAPTER NINETEEN:

JESUS IS OUR INTERCESSOR

Have you ever felt like the pressure was so heavy, the fight so lopsided, the burden so big that you just couldn't make it through? Martin Luther did, too. He was prone to doubts. The great reformer could match the angels with his faith. At times, however, he could rival the atheists with his reservations.

One day he fell so low in spirit that his friends were frightened at what he might say or do. They convinced him to rest and retreat, but he emerged from his sabbatical looking as sour and gloomy as ever. His fervor had faded and his followers feared that he would abandon his work.

He might have done exactly that, except for the actions of his wife, Katharina. He went home to find her dressed in black, weeping as from a death in the house. By her side lay a mourning cloak, such as ladies wore at funerals. He begged for an explanation. "Kate, what matters now? Is the child dead?" She shook her head and said their little ones were alive, but something much worse than that had happened. Luther cried, "Oh, what has befallen us? Tell me quick! I am sad enough as it is. Tell me quick!"

"Good man," she replied, "have you not heard? Is it possible that the terrible news has not reached you?" He shook his weary head and pressed her for an explanation. She continued, "Have you not been told that our heavenly Father is dead, and His cause in the world is therefore overturned?"

Luther looked at her for the longest time and, at last, burst into such a laugh that he could not contain himself. "Kate," he said, "I read thy riddle—what a fool I am! God is not dead, He ever lives; but I have acted as if He were."

Luther can be forgiven for having his doubts. Every bridge of faith has been known to sway during times of storms. From Luther to Lucado, we have all had those moments. Moments where the storms rage and the waves threaten to overtake us. Waves of destruction, fear, depression, isolation, or addiction.

Maybe that is the reason the Gospels speak so often about Jesus in the midst of storms. We might assume they would have stopped. Jesus was on the earth, after all. He made the planet. He invented storm systems. He created the whole idea of atmosphere, winds, and rains. We might assume that, for the time He was on His earth, the world would have been storm-free; that God would suspend the laws of nature and spare His Son the discomfort of slashing rains and howling winds. Jesus should be spared the storms of life. And so should we.

To follow Jesus is to live a storm-free life, right?

That expectation is quick to crash on the rocks of reality. The truth of the matter is this: Life comes with storms. It does for you. It does for me. It did for Jesus. Yet in the midst of these storms there is a powerful promise available to believers that we can hold on to tighter than any life raft.

Romans 8:34 (NIV):

Jesus is at _____ **of God and is also** _____ for us.

Have you heard this promise? It is a promise that takes the pressure off your shoulders, wipes the sweat from your brow, and reminds you that you are not going through the storms of life alone.

When Tyler Sullivan was an eleven-year-old elementary school student, he skipped a day of class. He played hooky, not in order to hang out with friends or watch television, he missed school so he could meet the President of the United States.

Barack Obama was visiting Tyler's hometown of Golden Valley, Minnesota. His father would introduce the president at an event. After the speech, when Tyler met the president, Obama realized that Tyler was missing school. He asked an aide for a pen and a card with presidential letterhead. He asked for the name of Tyler's teacher. He then wrote a note: "Please excuse Tyler. He was with me. Barack Obama, President"

I am thinking that the teacher read the note and granted the request. It is not every day that the president speaks up on behalf of a kid.

But you have more. The King of the universe is speaking for you. You can be sure, when Jesus speaks, all of heaven listens.

In the midst of any storm, trial, or tribulation, you do not have to ask where Jesus is or what He is doing.

You are not forgotten.

You are not alone.

You are not abandoned.

You will not be shipwrecked.

You have someone very powerful on your side. He sees you and is making your case known.

GOD'S PROMISE:

Jesus is ever praying for you.

> ## MY PROMISE:
>
> *I will take heart because Jesus is speaking up for me.*

Jesus understands storms. He went through His own. So did the disciples who were with Him.

Matthew tells the story of Jesus sending His disciples out onto the waters ahead of Him, on what turned out to be one particularly stormy night, while He stayed behind to dismiss the crowd.

Sometimes we create our own storms. We drink too much liquor or borrow too much money or hang out with the wrong crowd. We find ourselves is a storm of our own making.

This was not the case with the disciples. They were on the sea and in the storm because Christ bade them to be there. "Jesus made the disciples get into the boat…" This was not Jonah seeking to escape God; these were disciples seeking to obey God.

These are missionaries who move overseas, only to have support evaporate; business leaders who take the high road, only to see their efforts outbid by the dishonest. When a couple honors God in marriage only to have an empty crib; a student studies, only to fall short on the exam. When disciples sail in a boat that Jesus launched, only to sail into a storm, we are reminded that storms come even to the obedient. And they come with a punch.

Matthew 14:23 (NIV) says:

After Jesus had dismissed the people, he went up on a mountainside

_____ to pray. When evening came, he was there _____,
but the boat with the disciples was already a considerable distance from
land, buffeted by the waves because _____.

Storms can be fierce on the Sea of Galilee. During the autumn and
winter months, cold maritime air pushes into the Mediterranean basin and
collides with a tropical air mass. This creates eddies of low pressure storms
that funnel out of the ravines into the Galilean basin, which sits 682 feet
below the level of the Mediterranean.

Matthew was careful to count the hours of the ordeal. Jesus dismissed
the crowd and launched the disciples at the evening hour. We do not know
what time the storm hit, but we do know that John says the disciples had
rowed "three or four miles" (John 6:19). They had left the eastern shore
when darkness fell or soon thereafter. The night deepened. Hour upon hour
passed. Evening became night, night became windy and rainy, and before
long their boat was riding the raging roller coaster of the Galilean sea. The
five-mile trip should have taken them less than an hour, but at three a.m.
they were still far from the shore. The storm showed no sign of letting up.

Let us climb in the boat with the disciples. Look into their rain-splattered
faces. What do you see? Fear, for sure. Doubt? Absolutely. You may even hear
a question. Shouting over the wind, someone asks, "Does anyone know
where Jesus is?"

Now, let's give the disciples a little credit. They did not turn about and
return to the shore, but they persisted in obedience. They kept digging the
oars into the water and pulling the craft across the sea. In the pecking order
of the night, the storm called the shots. But the disciples were too far from
the shore, too long in the struggle, and too small in the waves.

And you? Do you feel too far from the shore? No solution in sight. Too
long in the struggle? Too long in the court-system? Too long in the doctor's

office? Too long without a good friend? Too long and too lonely? Too small against the waves?

Where is Jesus when you need Him?

Where was He the night of the storm in Galilee? When the ferocious storm was pounding on the obedient disciples, where in the world was Jesus?

The answer is clear. He was praying.

Matthew writes that Jesus had gone up on a mountainside by Himself to pray. There is no indication that Jesus did anything else. He did not eat. He did not chat. He did not sleep. He prayed. Jesus was so intent in prayer that He refused to stop even though His skin was soaked and hair was matted. After He served all day, He prayed all night. He felt the gale force winds and the skin-stinging rain. He was in the storm but still He prayed.

Or should we say, He was in the storm, and so He prayed? Was the storm the reason for His intercession? And… Do the disciples represent all His followers? Does the storm represent all tough times and do His actions describe His first course of action…to pray for His followers? For the promise in Romans 8:34 tells us, He is "at the right hand of God and is also interceding for us."

To "intercede" means to make specific requests or petitions before someone. This is what intercessors do. They offer a passionate and specific request before God.

Ponder this promise for a moment. Jesus, right now, at this moment, in the midst of your storm, is interceding for you. The King of the universe is speaking up on your behalf. He is calling out to the heavenly Father. He is urging the help of the Holy Spirit. He is advocating for a special blessing to be sent your way.

"Grant Mary the strength to face this interview!"

"Issue to Tom the wisdom necessary to be a good father!"

"Defeat the fear that seeks to rob Allison of her sleep!"

Where is Jesus? Peter and crew may have asked.

Where is Jesus? The bedridden, enfeebled, impoverished, overstressed, isolated ask.

Where is Jesus? He is in the presence of God, praying for us.

Hebrews 7:25 (NIV) states:

Therefore he is able to _____ those who come to God through him, because he _____ for them.

When we forget to pray, He remembers to pray. When we are full of doubt, He is full of faith.

Where we are unworthy to be heard, He is ever worthy to be heard. He is the sinless and perfect high priest. The King of the universe is speaking for you. In the midst of your storm, He is praying.

And, through the midst of your storm, He is coming.

Matthew goes on to tell the rest of the story:

During the fourth watch of the night Jesus _____, walking on the lake. When the disciples saw him _____, they were terrified. "It is a ghost," they said, and _____ (Matthew 14:25–26 NIV).

Jesus became the answer to His own prayer. Jesus did not still the storm and then appear. He appeared in the midst of the storm. He commanded the torrent to become a trail and the sea to become solid. He, who made two walls out of the Red Sea for Moses and the iron ax to swim for Elisha, treated the water of Galilee like a mountain path and came walking to the apostles in the storm.

Still the followers panicked. They never expected to see Jesus in the storm. His followers thought He was a ghost at first. But Jesus stayed. Peter's faith became fear, but Jesus stayed. The winds howled and raged...but Jesus stayed. He stayed until His point was made. He is sovereign over all storms.

The disciples, for the first time in recorded Scripture, worshiped Him. They said, "Truly, You are the Son of God" (vs. 33). With stilled boat as their altar and beating hearts as their liturgy, they worshipped Jesus.

And that could be end of the story, and a wonderful ending at that. But Matthew makes sure that we find out what happened on the other side of that storm.

After they had crossed over, the people recognized Jesus. The news of His arrival spread quickly throughout the whole area, and soon people were bringing all their sick. We are told, "All who touched him were healed" (vs.36).

On the other side of the storm were more miracles than could be counted. What would have happened if the disciples had turned around and gone back? Jesus probably would have still visited those people, but the disciples would have missed out on being a part of it. They would have been sitting on the other side. Maybe catching some fish off the shore to pass the time. And perhaps a little sullenly wondering why they weren't experiencing the miracles.

But instead, the disciples were right there in the midst of it all! And they would have a story to tell around campfires for years to come...the night Jesus came walking on the water...the night Jesus rescued them in the midst of the storm.

What storm are you facing? However dark and windy, however violent and threatening, you can build your life on this promise. **Jesus is interceding for you**. And then make your own promise:

I will take heart because Jesus is speaking up for me.

QUESTIONS FOR REFLECTION:

1. Why do you think Jesus waited until the storm was at its worst to approach the disciples?

_____

_____

_____

_____

2. If you are in midst of a storm in your life, does it comfort you to know Jesus is praying for you?

_____

_____

_____

_____

_____

3. At first, the disciples did not recognize Jesus. They thought He was a ghost. How can you be sure Jesus is with you in the storms of life?

_____

_____

_____

_____

_____

CHAPTER TWENTY:

GOD DOES NOT CONDEMN

On a splendid April afternoon in 2008, two college women's softball teams squared off beneath the blue sky of the Cascade Mountains.

Inside a chainlink fence before a hundred fans, the two teams played a decisive game. The winner would advance to the division playoffs. The Western Oregon Wolves were a sturdy team that boasted several strong batters, but Sara Tucholsky was not one of them. Sara had never hit a home run in her life, but on that Saturday, with two runners on base, she connected with a curveball and sent it sailing over the left field fence.

In her excitement, Sara overstepped first base. Pivoting back, something popped in her knee and down she went. She pulled herself back to the bag, pulled her knee to her chest in pain, and asked the umpire, "What do I do?"

The umpire was not sure. If any of Sara's teammates assisted her, she would be out. Sara knew this much: if she tried to stand, she would collapse. Her team couldn't help her. Her leg couldn't support her. How could Sara cross home plate?

The umpires huddled to talk. And while they huddle and Sara groans, can I make a comparison? Blame it on the preacher in me, but I see an illustration in this moment. You and I have a lot in common with Sara Tucholsky. We, too, have stumbled. Not in baseball, but in life: in morality, honesty, integrity. We have done our best only to trip and fall. Our finest efforts have left us flat on our backs, in the dust, and out of the game. The distance between where we are and where we want to be is impassable. What do we do?

As the apostle Paul writes in Romans 3:10–11, "There is no one righteous, not even one; there is no one who understands; there is no one who seeks God." People often bristle at the message of this verse. They take offense at its allegation. "No one is righteous? No one seeks God?" And how often do we produce our own resume of righteousness? *I pay my taxes! I love my family! I do not drink all that much! By most standards, I am a good person!*

Besides, we reason, *at least I am not as bad as...* and the list begins: an evil dictator, a mass murderer, a slimy politician, a reality show contestant...

I tried that approach with my mom once. She told me that my room was messy. I showed her my brother's room. I could always count on his to be messier than mine. She walked me down the hall to her room. It was spotless! No wrinkle on the bed. No clothing on the floor. Perfect! "This is what I mean by clean," she said.

God does the same with our excuses—He points to His Son and says: "This is what I mean by perfect."

So much for our excuses. We are left where Sara Tucholsky was—unable to stand on our own two feet.

The amazing news is Jesus did for us what Mallory Holtman did for Sara. When we last saw Sara, she was lying on the ground, clinging to her knee with one hand and first base with the other. The umpires huddled. The players stood and watched. The fans shouted for someone to take Sara off the field, but she wanted to cross home plate for her team. She had just knocked the ball out of the park! But she just was not strong enough. She couldn't do it on her own.

Mallory Holtman, who played first base for the opposing team, came up with a solution. A loss would end the season of her senior year. So, you would think Mallory would be happy to see the homerun nullified. She was not.

Asking permission, she signaled for the shortstop to help her, and they picked up the injured player, tears streaming down Sara's face. The mission of mercy began. They carried her around the bases, touching each along the way. The spectators rose to their feet and cheered.

Mallory's solution was the perfect solution. Through her efforts, the standard of the game was honored and the desire of the player was rewarded. The only one who could help, did help. And, because she did, Sara made it home.

God offers to do the same for you and me. No matter how big the fall, how messy the mess, and how broken you feel, He says, "I will pick you up and carry you home." He does so, through the finished work of Jesus Christ on the cross.

God's beautiful promise to us is this:

There is now _____ for those who are in _____ (Romans 8:1 NIV).

GOD'S PROMISE:

I will not condemn you if you believe in My Son.

> ## MY PROMISE:
>
> *I will find forgiveness in the finished work of Christ.*

When you hear "cross," what comes to your mind? A slender symbol hanging from a gold chain? An ornamental fixture atop a church steeple? Maybe a heavy wooden crucifix nailed above a podium? The cross represents many things to many people: religion, sacraments, Sunday school, Grandma's Bible. And the feelings are just as varied. For some it brings up feelings of antipathy and condemnation. For others, a sense of freedom and redemption.

For one man what started as a fire that fueled his hate for the cross became the fire that fueled his greatest passion.

He once considered himself a Pharisee of all Pharisees, the most religious man in town. But all his scruples and law keeping hadn't made him into a better man. Saul was bloodthirsty and angry, determined to extinguish anything and everyone Christian. The first time we are introduced to him, he's overseeing the death of Steven, who is being stoned for his faith.

However, Saul's attitude began to change on the road to Damascus. That's when Jesus appeared to him. Jesus, the One who had died, nailed to a cross. The One whose name was whispered along with "resurrected," and "the Son of God." The One whose followers Saul had been determined to wipe out.

Jesus knocked Saul off his high horse (literally), and left him alone and sightless for three days. Saul could only see one direction: inward. And what he saw he did not like. He saw a narrow-minded tyrant. When he was told that he could be baptized and wash away his sins, he did not wait for a second invitation.

Within a few days, he was preaching about Christ and the cross. Within a few years, he was off on his first missionary journey. Within a decade, he was writing the letters that we still read today, each one making the case for Christ and the cross. Saul became Paul, author of a third of our New Testament.

We are not told when Paul realized the meaning of grace. Was it immediately on the Damascus Road? Or gradually during the three-day darkness? We are not told. But we know this: Paul got it.

He embraced the improbable offer that God would make us right with Himself through the forgiveness of sins, through Jesus Christ and His sacrifice on the cross. And Paul made the grace of Christ his life message.

He preached:

For all have _____ and _____ of the glory of God (Romans 3:23 NIV).

We have not met the standard God set. According to the Garden of Eden plan, we were made in God's image. We were intended to bear the nature of God. To speak, act, and behave like He speaks, acts, and behaves. To love like He loves. To value what He values. To honor whom He honors. This is the "glorious standard" God has set.

Yet, a yawning canyon separates us from God. He is holy; we are not. He is perfect; we are not. So what are we to do? If we cannot deny our sin, might we hope that God will overlook it? He would, except for this one essential detail. He is a God of justice.

He will punish our sin. He must. If He does not, He is not just. If He is not just, then what hope do we have of a just heaven? God must punish sin or He is not just. Yet, if God punishes sinners, then we are lost. So what is the solution? Again, we turn to Paul for the explanation:

Paul recognized that were it not for Christ, and the price He paid for our sins, we could never be righteous. He penned this in one of his letters he wrote to the Romans. He wrote:

God presented Christ as a sacrifice of _____, through the shedding of his blood—to be received _____. He did this to demonstrate his righteousness, because in his forbearance he had left the sins committed beforehand unpunished—he did it to demonstrate his righteousness at the present time, so as to be _____ and _____ those who have faith in Jesus (Romans 3:25–26 NIV).

God never compromised His standard. He satisfied every demand of justice. Yet, He also gratified the longing of love. He was too just to overlook our sin, too loving to dismiss us, so He placed our sin on His Son and punished it there. Jesus took our sin on the cross, paying the price for Paul, for you, for me.

Now we understand the cry of Christ from the cross. "My God, my God, why have you forsaken me?" Jesus felt the deep and furious wrath of a just and holy God. We are not unacquainted with this wrath. God allows us to experience just a drop of the tidal wave of shame and misery that our sins deserve. He permits a grain of guilt, while we deserve a mountain, in order to bring us to repentance. Can you imagine if we felt the full weight of our sin?

Jesus did. Wave after wave. Load after load. Hour after hour. He felt the separation between Him and His Father. And then when He could scarcely take any more, He cried: "It is finished!" The mission was complete.

At the moment of Jesus' death, an unbelievable miracle occurred.

Jesus cried out with a loud voice, and breathed His last. Then the _____ was torn in two from _____ (Mark 15:37–38 NKJV).

A thick veil, six feet long and thirty feet wide, separated the people and their sin from the temple's Most Holy Place where they came to worship God. We are not talking about small delicate drapes. This curtain was a wall made of fabric. The fact that it was torn from top to bottom reveals that the Hands behind the deed were divine. It was God Himself who took it upon Himself to grasp the curtain and rip it in two.

No more!

No more division.

No more separation.

No more sacrifices.

It was finished. Christ's death brought new life. Every obstacle that had separated—and could ever separate—us from God was gone.

The promise is written with the crimson blood of Christ: "There is now no condemnation for those who are in Christ Jesus" (Romans 8:1).

No condemnation. Not "limited condemnation," "appropriate condemnation," "calculated condemnation." That is what people give people. What does God give His children? "No condemnation."

Jesus was truly the Lamb of God who took away the sins of the world. Only Jesus could help us, for only Jesus was sinless. First Peter 2:24 tells us:

He personally carried _____ in his body on the cross so we can be _____ and live for what is right (NIV).

Jesus bore the weight of our sin.

Salvation, from beginning to end, is a work of our Father. God does not stand on a mountain and tell us to climb it and find Him. He comes down into our dark valley and finds us. He does not offer to complete the work if we will start it. He does all the work, from beginning to end. He does not bargain with us, telling us to clean up our lives so he can help. He washes our sins without our help. When you place your trust in Christ, He places His arms around you. He carries you home. Scripture says God is able to "keep you from falling and to present you before his glorious presence without fault and with great joy" (Jude 24 NIV).

We need this promise. We fall; we fall in our lust, our anger, our addictions. We fall face-first, so publicly, so undeniably that we despair of ever rising again. It is in those moments that only the promise of God can save us.

No condemnation.

Frustration? Yes.

Temptation? A-plenty.

Humiliation? For sure.

But condemnation? Cut off from God? Divorced from all hope? No, no, a thousand times no!

The cross is not a symbol of condemnation. The cross is a symbol of hope, freedom, and forgiveness. A constant reminder that our sin has been paid for, once and for all.

Like Paul who wrote this powerful promise, we too can hold to it: "There is now no condemnation for those who are in Christ Jesus." And because of this, we can say with unshakable confidence:

I will find forgiveness in the finished work of Christ.

QUESTIONS FOR REFLECTION:

1. What is the difference between condemnation and conviction? Between guilt and the true knowledge of sin?

_____

_____

_____

_____

2. First John 3:20 says, "If our hearts condemn us, we know that God is greater than our hearts, and he knows everything." How do you see this worked out in a practical way in your life?

_____

_____

_____

_____

_____

_____

3. Jesus cried from the cross, "It is finished." What did Jesus finish?

_____

_____

_____

_____

CHAPTER TWENTY-ONE:

JESUS GIVES VICTORY OVER DEATH

If you have attended a memorial service, you have heard the words. If you have walked through a cemetery, you have read them. They are quoted at the gravesides of paupers, carved on the headstones of kings. Those who know nothing of the Bible know this part of the Bible. Those who quote no Scripture can remember this Scripture, the one about the valley and the shadow and the shepherd.

Yea, though I walk through the valley of the _____, I will fear no evil; for You are with me; Your rod and Your staff, they comfort me (Psalm 23:4 NKJV).

Why? Why are these words so treasured? Why is this verse so beloved? David, who often faced death at every turn, grants us an important reminder that helps us surrender our fear of the grave.

We all have to face it. In a life marked by doctor appointments, dentist appointments, and school appointments, there is one appointment that none of us will miss: the appointment with death. Several years ago, I received an urgent call to visit a dying man in the hospital. I did not know Peter well, but well enough to know that he was paying a high price for his hard living. Years of drugs and alcohol abuse had perforated his system. Though he would make peace with God through Christ, his liver was at conflict with his body.

When his ex-wife phoned me, she was standing at his bedside. Peter, she explained, was knocking at death's door. Though I hurried, he entered it seconds before I arrived. The hospital room atmosphere had a "just happened" feel to it. She was still standing by the bed. His hair was stroked back from her touch. The imprint of a lipstick kiss was just below the knuckles on his left hand. Perspiration beads sparkled on his forehead.

She saw me enter and looked up. With her eyes and words she explained, "He just left." He silently slipped out. Exited. Departed. One moment here. The next moment…where? He passed, not away, but on.

Yet on to where? And in what form? To what place? In what manner? And, once there, what did he see? Know or do? We so desire to know.

Who in your life "just left"? When the breathing of your husband ceased, the beating heart in your womb stopped, when the beep of your grandmother's monitor became a flat-lined tone, what happened in that moment? Death is hard for us to face. Especially when it seems like the ultimate end. But what if death were more like the end of a wonderful movie before you put in the sequel, rather than the dead-end of a long road?

Hebrews 9:27 tells us:

Everyone must _____, and after that be judged by God (NIV).

Oh, how we would like to change that verse. Just a word or two would suffice. "Nearly everyone must die…" or "Everyone *but me* must die…" or "Everyone who forgets to eat right and take vitamins must die…" But those are not God's words. In His plan everyone must die, even those who eat right and take their vitamins.

The wise remember the brevity of life. Exercise may buy us a few more heartbeats. Medicine may grant us a few more breaths. But in the end, there is an end. And, what will happen to you in your final moment? Barring the return of Christ, you will have one last gasp, a final pulse. Your lungs will empty and blood will still. When asked the question, "What will we be after we die?" the human race has conjured up four answers.

Option 1: Nothing. We will decay or disintegrate. Death is a dead end. Our works and reputation might survive, but not us.

Option 2: Ghosts. Phantoms of what we once were. Pale as Edgar Winters' beard. Structured as a morning mist. What will we be after we die? Specters.

Option 3: Hawks, or cows, or a car mechanic in Kokomo. Reincarnation rewards or punishes us according to our behavior. We come back to earth in another mortal body.

Or, Option 4: We will become part of the universe. Eternity absorbs us like a lake absorbs a storm. We return to what we were before we were what we are… we return to the cosmic consciousness of the universe.

Christianity, on the other hand, posits a new, startling, surprising idea. What you had before death, you'll have after death, only better, much, much better. It says you will go to paradise: heaven, but not home. Upon the return of Christ, you will receive a spiritual body and inhabit a restored universe. This is the promise of God.

And the best way to face death is to claim the promise of God in 1 Corinthians 15:54 (NIV):

_____ has been _____ in victory.

We believe this promise because of the resurrection of Jesus.

> ## GOD'S PROMISE:
>
> *I will not condemn you if you believe in My Son.*

> ## MY PROMISE:
>
> *I will find forgiveness in the finished work of Christ.*

Jesus had been crucified, the disciples scattered, the stone rolled in place. It looked like it was over. Death had come. Death had won. But this was not the end. Matthew 28:2–6 (NIV) puts it this way:

There was a violent earthquake, for an _____ came down from heaven and, going to the tomb, _____ _____ and sat on it. His appearance was like lightning, and his clothes were white as snow. The guards were so afraid of him that they shook and became like dead men. The angel said to the women, "_____, for I know that you are looking for Jesus, who was crucified. He is _____; he has _____, just as he said. Come and see the place where he lay."

The resurrection changed everything. Had such words never been spoken, had the body of Jesus decayed into dust in the borrowed tomb, you would not be listening to these words and we would not be discussing this promise. But the words were spoken and the promise was made.

His resurrection is the promise of ours. What God did for Jesus, He will do with us. According to the apostle Paul, when Jesus rose from the dead, He was the "first fruits." (See I Corinthians 15:20–23.) "First fruits" is the first taste of the harvest. The farmer can anticipate the nature of the crop by sampling the first crop. We can anticipate our own resurrection by trusting the empty tomb of Christ. Because Jesus conquered death and the grave, death is no longer the end.

In Revelation, Jesus says that He now holds the keys to both death and the grave. He said:

"I am the _____ one. I _____, but look—I am _____ forever and ever! And I hold the keys of _____ " (Revelation 1:18 NIV).

In other words, He set us free from its power, its hold on us. No longer does it have the control. No longer does death have the final say. The One who defeated the grave defeated it for us as well. Death is no longer something to be feared.

Here is what is going to happen to you. Upon death, your spirit will immediately enter into the presence of God. You will enjoy conscious fellowship with the Father and with those who have gone before.

Is not this the promise that Jesus gave the thief on the cross? "Today you will be with me in paradise" (Luke 23:43). The first word of the sentence declares the instant transfer from this life to the next. "Today," Christ promises. No delay. No pause. No purgatory cleansing or soul sleeping. The thief closed his eyes on earth and awoke in paradise. The soul of the believer journeys home, while the body of the believer awaits the resurrection. Paradise is the first stage of heaven.

But paradise is not the final version of heaven, nor the ultimate expression of home.

The final age will begin when Christ returns on the final day. The day will begin with a shout. Scripture says:

For the _____ will descend from heaven with a _____(1 Thessalonians 4:16 NKJV).

Before you see angels, hear trumpets, or embrace your grandparents, you will be engulfed by Jesus' voice.

Jesus described it this way:

"The _____ will hear the voice of the Son of God...all who are... in their _____ will hear his voice...they will _____" (John 5: 25, 28–29 NCV).

He who created us will collect us. We will be resurrected from our graves —our bodies joined with our spirits.

You are going to love your new version of you! You will finally be healthy. According to First John: ...we know that when he _____, we will be _____ (1 John 3:2).

Let every parent of a Down syndrome or autistic child write these words on the bedroom wall.

Let the amputees and infected, bed-ridden and anemic put themselves to sleep with the promise, "We shall be like Him." Let the wheelchair-bound and atrophied take this promise to heart. "We shall be like Him." We shall graduate from this version to His likeness. We shall enjoy a body like His, made for heaven and earth.

Not only will disease be gone; sin will be gone as well. As much as we hate carcinoma and cardiac arrests, do not we hate jealousy even more? Cystic fibrosis steals breath, but selfishness and stinginess steal joy. Diabetes can ruin the system of a body, but deceit, denial, and distrust are ruining society.

In the new Kingdom, our eyes won't lust, our minds won't wander, our hands won't steal, our hearts won't judge, our appetites won't rage, and our tongues won't lie.

But what we will be, will be spiritual.

Let this hope for tomorrow bring strength to today. Some of you indwell such road-weary bodies: knees ache, eyes dim, skin sags. Others of you exited the womb on an uphill ride. While I have no easy answers for your struggle, I invite, no, I *implore* you to stand with me on the promise of Paul:

"Death has been swallowed up in victory" (I Cor. 15:54 NIV).

Several weeks ago, I spent an hour in the office of a cemetery director. Yet another birthday had reminded me that the day of my departure is increasingly near. It seemed right to me to make burial preparations.

As the gentleman was showing me the funeral map and the available sections, I had an idea. "You'll likely think I am crazy," I told him. "But can I record a message for my tombstone? A sort of voice mail for the grave."

To his credit, he did not call me crazy and promised to check. Within a few days he gave me the good news, "Yes, it is possible. A recorded message can be encased in the grave-marker. At the push of the button, a message can be played."

I thanked him and got to work. Within a few minutes, I had it written. It is not yet recorded.

Perhaps I can test it with you first? The granite stone will contain a button and an invitation: "Press for a word from Max." If you do, here is what you'll hear.

Thanks for coming by. Sorry you missed me. I am not here. I am home. Finally, home. At some point my King will call and this grave will be shown for the temporary tomb it is. You might want to step to the side, in case that happens while you are here. Again, I appreciate the visit. Hoping you have made plans for your own departure. All the best, Max.

Yeah, it still needs some work. While the wording might change, the promise never will:

"Death has been swallowed up in victory" (1 Corinthians 15:54).

The ground shook. The stone was rolled away. Jesus is alive! Death is nothing to be feared. Therefore we can make our own confident promise in this unshakable hope.

"I will entrust my death to the Lord of life."

QUESTIONS FOR REFLECTION:

1. Many people spend so much time and energy avoiding death that they miss the chance to fully live. Why do you think this is?

_____

_____

_____

_____

2. Who do you have in your life to carry you around the bases when you cannot stand on your own?

_____

_____

_____

_____

_____

_____

3. How should believers live knowing that death in this world is not the end of their life?

_____

_____

_____

_____

_____

PRAYING THE PROMISE:

Jesus, thank You for swallowing up my death in Your death.
You have robbed the grave of sorrow.
The cross has conquered my fear.
I trust You with my life,
because You are the giver of life,
and life more abundant.
Help me to live out my days with eternity in mind.
In Your name, I pray.
Amen.

Chapter Twenty-Two:

Joy Comes in the Morning

My friend, I have good news for you. Now, listen carefully. No matter how dark the night may seem, no matter how distraught your heart may be, God loves you. And because He does, you can be assured joy WILL come.

Mary Cushman learned this truth. The financial Depression of the 1930s all but devastated her family. Her husband's paycheck shrank to eighteen dollars a week. Since he was given to illness, there were many weeks that he did not even earn that much.

She began to take in laundry and ironing. She dressed her five kids with cast-off clothing. At one point the local grocer, to whom they owed fifty dollars, accused her eleven-year-old son of stealing.

That was all she could take. She could see no hope. So she shut off her washing machine and took her beautiful little five-year-old girl in to the bedroom, plugged up the window and cracks, and turned on the gas heater in her bedroom. She did not light it. Instead, she told her daughter they were going to take a nap and lay down to take her last. She said later that she would never forget the smell of that gas.

Suddenly, she heard music. She had forgotten to turn the radio off in the kitchen. As the music continued she heard someone singing an old hymn.

What a friend we have in Jesus
All our sins and grief to bear
What a privilege to carry
Everything to God in prayer

Oh, what peace we often forfeit Oh what needless pain we bear
All because we do not carry
Everything to God in prayer

As she listened to the hymn, she suddenly realized she had made a terrible and tragic mistake. She had tried to fight all her battles alone. Jumping up, she turned off the gas, opened the door, and raised her windows to let in the fresh air.

She spent the rest of the day giving thanks to God for the blessings she had forgotten: five healthy children. She promised that she would never be ungrateful and acknowledge God in the midst of the darkness. They eventually lost their home, but she never lost her hope. They weathered the Depression. Those five children grew up, married, and had children of their own.

She wrote, "As I look back on that terrible day when I turned on the gas, I thank God over and over that I woke up in time. What joys I would have missed. How many wonderful years I would have forfeited forever... Whenever I hear now of someone who wants to end his life I feel like crying out, 'Do not do it! Do not!' The blackest moments we live through can only last a little time—and then comes the future..."

Have your nights been filled with tears? Dear one, I have a beautiful and hope-filled promise to share with you.

_____ may last through the night, but _____comes with the morning (Psalm 30:5 NIV).

You did not need to read that verse to know its truth. Weeping can last through the night. Just ask the widow in the cemetery, or the mother in the emergency room. The man who lost his job can tell you. So can the teenager who lost her way. Weeping may last through the night, and the next night and the next. This is not news to you.

But despair will not rule the day. Sorrow will not last forever. The clouds may eclipse the sun but they cannot eliminate it. Night might prolong the dawn, but it cannot defeat it. Morning comes. Not as quickly as we want. Not as soon as we desire. But morning comes and with it comes joy.

We have this precious promise to hold on to:

Weeping may last through the night, but joy comes with the morning.

Do you need that promise? Have you wept a river? Have you forsaken all hope? Do you wonder if a morning will ever bring this night to an end? Joys comes. Watch for it. Wait for it. Expect it like you would the morning sunrise or the evening twilight. It came to Mary Cushman. And it will come to you, my friend.

GOD'S PROMISE:

Your night will come to an end; there will be joy in the morning.

My Promise:

I will praise God before my prayer is answered.

In the forest of the New Testament, she is the weeping willow. She is the one upon whom tragedy cast its coldest winter. Before she knew Jesus, she had seven demons. She was a prisoner of seven afflictions. What might this list include? Depression? Loneliness? Shame? Fear? Perhaps she was a recluse or a prostitute. Maybe she would been abused, abandoned. The number seven is sometimes used in the Bible to describe completeness. It could be that Mary Magdalene was completely consumed with troubles.

But then something happened. Jesus stepped into her world. Jesus spoke and the demons fled. With one word, the oppressive forces were gone. Banished. Evicted. For the first time in a long time, Mary Magdalene could sleep well, eat enough, smile again. The face in the mirror was not anguished. Jesus restored life to her life.

She reciprocated. We read that she was among the female followers who were contributing from their own resources to support Jesus and His disciples. Wherever Jesus went, Mary Magdalene followed. She heard him teach. She saw Him perform miracles. She helped pay expenses. She may have even prepared His meals. She was always near Christ.

Even at His crucifixion. She was the one who stood near the cross. When they pounded the nails in His hands, she heard the hammer. When they pierced His side with a spear, she saw the blood. When they lowered His body from the cross, she was there to help prepare it for burial.

On Friday, Mary Magdalene watched Jesus die.

On Saturday, she observed a sad Sabbath.

When Sunday came, Mary Magdalene went to the tomb to finish the work she had begun on Friday. John 20:1 says that early on the first day of the week, Mary Magdalene went to the tomb while it was still dark. She knew nothing of the empty tomb. She came with no other motive except to wash the remaining clots of blood from His beard and say good-bye.

As she carried the perfume for His burial, memories returned to her of an evening past, when she had been compelled to pour her precious perfume on His feet, washing them with her tears and wiping them with her hair. He had changed her life. He had changed everything. And now...

Before, she carried the perfume to Jesus with a grateful, worshipful heart. Now she carried the perfume to Jesus with a grief-stricken, sorrowful heart.

It was a dark morning.

When she arrived at the cemetery, the bad news became worse. She saw that the stone had been rolled away and assumed that grave robbers had taken the body. She hurried back down the trail until she found Peter and John, and told them, "They've taken away the Lord out of the tomb" (John 20:2).

Peter and John ran to the gravesite. John was faster but Peter was bolder. He stepped inside. John followed him. Peter saw the empty slab and stared. But John saw the empty slab and believed. The evidence all came together for him. The resurrection prophecies, the removed stone, the linen wrappings, the head cloth folded and placed. John did the math. No one took Jesus' body. No one robbed the grave. Jesus rose from the dead. John looked and believed. Easter had its first celebrant. Peter and John hurried to tell the others.

We expect the camera lens of the gospel to follow them. After all, they were apostles, authors of epistles. They comprise two-thirds of the inner circle. We expect John to describe what the apostles did next. He does not. He tells the story of the one who remained behind.

Scripture says, "Mary stood outside by the tomb weeping" (John 20:11). Her face was awash with tears. Her shoulders heaved with sobs. She felt all alone. It was just Mary Magdalene, her despair, and a vacant tomb. As she wept, she stooped down and looked into the tomb. And she saw two angels in white sitting, one at the head and the other at the feet, where the body of Jesus had lain. Then they said to her, 'Woman, why are you weeping?'" (vs. 11–12)

Mary Magdalene mistook the angels for men. It is easy to imagine why. It was still dark outside, even darker in the tomb. Her eyes were tear-filled. She had no reason to think that angels would be in the tomb. Bone-diggers? Maybe. Caretakers? Possibly. But her Sunday was too dark to expect the presence of angels. She answered, "They have taken away my Lord, and I do not know where they have laid him" (vs.13).

Mary's world officially hit rock bottom. Her master was murdered. His body was buried in a borrowed grave. His tomb was robbed. His body was stolen. Now, two strangers were sitting on the slab where his body had been laid. Sorrow intermingled with anger.

Have you ever had a moment like this? A moment in which bad news became worse? In which the sadness wrapped around you like a fog? In which you came looking for God yet couldn't find Him? Maybe Mary Magdalene's story is your story. If so, you are going to love what happened next. In the midst of Mary's darkest moment, the Son came out.

Now when she had said this, she turned around and saw Jesus standing there, and did not know that it was Jesus. We read:

Jesus said to her, "Woman, why are you weeping? Whom are you seeking?" She, _____, said to

Him, **"Sir, if you have carried Him away, tell me where you have laid Him and I will take Him away"** (John 20:14–15 NIV).

She did not recognize her Lord. So Jesus did something about it. He called her by name. He said to her, "Mary."

Maybe it was the way He said it. The inflection. The tone. The Galilean accent. Maybe it was the memory associated with it; the moment she first heard someone say her name without perversion or agenda.

"Mary."

When she heard the voice she knew the source. She turned around and cried out, "Rabbi." In a second, in a pivot of the neck, in the amount of time it took her to rotate her head from this way to that, her world went from dead Jesus to a living one. Weeping may last through the night, but joy… She threw her arms around Him. We know this to be true because of the next words Jesus said:

"Do not _____, because I have not yet gone up to the Father" (vs. 17).

Maybe she fell at His feet and held His ankles.

Maybe she threw her arms around His shoulders and held Him close.

We do not know how she held Him. We just know she did.

And Jesus let her do so. How wonderful that the resurrected Lord was not too holy, too otherly, too divine, and too supernatural to be hugged.

Someone should paint this scene. Capture it in oil and frame it on canvas. The brilliant golden sunrise. The open tomb. Angels watching from a distance. The white-robed Messiah. The joy-filled Mary. Her arms around Him. His eyes upon her. If you are the artist who paints it, please include the reflection of the sunrise in the tears of Mary. And, by all means, paint a broad smile on the face of Jesus.

The story continues this way, "Then, Mary Magdalene went and told the disciples that she had seen the Lord and that he had spoken these things to her." Why? Why her? As far as we know, she did not become a missionary. No epistle bears her name. No New Testament story describes her work. Why did Jesus create this moment for Mary Magdalene?

Perhaps to send this message to all heavy-hearted people:

Weeping may last through the night, but joy comes with the morning (see Psalm 30:5).

Are you weeping? Do what Mary did. Keep coming to Jesus. Even though the trail is dark.

Even though the sun seems to sleep. Even though everyone else is silent, you walk to Jesus. Mary Magdalene did this. No, she did not comprehend the promise of Jesus. She came looking for a dead Jesus, not a living one. But at least she came. And because she came to Him, He came to her.

And you? You'll be tempted to give up and walk away. But do not. Even when you do not feel like it, keep walking the trail to the empty tomb. Open your Bible. Meditate on Scripture. Sing hymns. Talk to other believers. Place yourself in a position to be found by Jesus and listen carefully. That gardener very well might be your redeemer.

Weeping comes. It comes to all of us. Heartaches leave us with tear-streaked faces and heavy hearts. Weeping comes. But so does joy. Darkness comes, but so does the morning. Sadness comes, but so does hope.

No matter what in your life seems to be dead in the grave—your joy, your hope, your circumstances—put your trust in the God who brings the dead back to life. Sorrow may have the night, but it cannot have your life. Make this hope-filled promise with all that's within you:

"I will seek God even when I am sad."

Questions for Reflection:

1. Does God need us to stop weeping before we come to Him? (Hint: Read John 20.)

_____

_____

_____

_____

_____

_____

_____

2. In Mary's darkest hour, she went to be near Jesus. In a moment, Jesus turned her greatest sorrow into her greatest joy. How can you draw near to Jesus?

_____

_____

_____

_____

_____

_____

_____

_____

_____

PRAYING THE PROMISE:

Father, in Your creation You made seasons and days—summer and winter,
spring and fall, morning and night.

I may go through seasons that feel like nights,
but I trust that Your joy comes with the morning.
Help me to draw near to You, even when I am sad.
When sorrow tries to settle over me, remind me of Your promises of joy.
May I look to You always, even through my tears.
Amen.

CHAPTER TWENTY-THREE:

THE POWER OF THE HOLY SPIRIT IS FOR YOU

Several years ago, when my legs were stronger, belly was flatter, and ego was bigger, I let my friend Pat convince me to enter a bike race. Not just any bike race, mind you, but a race that included a one-and-a-half-mile pedal up a steep hill with a gradient of 12 percent. In other words, it was a tough, climb-out-of-the-saddle, set your thighs on fire, and prepare to suck air for ten-minute section of the race. Appropriately called The Killer Diller, and yes, it lived up to the hype.

I knew its reputation. Still, I signed up because Pat, my riding buddy, told me I could make it.

Easy for Pat to say. He is fifteen years my junior and has competed since his elementary school days. He was riding in pelotons before most of us knew what they were. When I balked at the idea of completing the race, he assured me, "Believe me, Max. You will make it."

I almost did not.

The riders who belonged there left those of us who did not far behind. We the barrel-bellied laggards made jokes about the upcoming ascent. But we did not joke for long. It takes wind to talk. We soon needed all the wind we could muster to climb. I pushed and huffed and puffed and, about that point, the ascent began. By the time I was halfway to the top my thighs were on fire and I was having less than pleasant thoughts about my friend Patrick.

That's when I felt the push. A hand was pressing against my back. I turned and looked. It was Pat! He had already completed the race. Anticipating my utter exhaustion, he had hurried back down the hill, dismounted his bike, and scurried to give me a hand. Literally. He began pushing me up the hill! (The fact that he could keep up with me tells you how slowly I was pedaling.) "I told you that you would make it," he shouted. "I came to make sure you did."

Feeling like you could use a little extra strength right now? Well God has a promise for that.

Acts 1:8 (NIV) says:

"You will receive_____ when the Holy Spirit comes on you."

Does the topic of the Holy Spirit puzzle you? Bewilder you? We feel comfortable discussing God the Father and God the Son, but God the Holy Spirit? Sometimes we avoid the discussion. We do so at great cost, however.

Suppose I offered you a deal on a shiny, new super-speed tricycle. Just think of the joy your youngster will have riding up and down the sidewalk on this spectacular trike. Fire-engine red. Tassels that dangle from the handles. And, listen to this, a little bell that sits on the handlebar. A great bargain. I am offering it at one third off the price. With these savings you can take the entire family out to dinner. Of course, there is the small matter of one missing wheel. But the trike still has two. Little Johnny will eventually need to ride a two-wheeler anyway, right? Might as well start him out right. Buy him this two-wheeled trike.

You are giving me a funny look. You are rolling your eyes at me like

Denalyn does. Now you are sighing. Come on, do not walk away. Think about it. One-third off the price for a trike that is missing one little tiny wheel. Do you not see the value here?

Of course you do not and I do not blame you. Who wants two-thirds when you can have the whole?

Many Christians do. Ask a believer to answer this question: *Who is God the Father?* They have a reply. *Describe God the Son.* They will not hesitate. But if you want to see them hem, haw, and search for words, ask this question: *Who is the Holy Spirit?* Even though the Holy Spirit occupies an equal third of the Trinity with the Father and the Son, it is as if we are settling for a two-thirds God. You wouldn't make that mistake with a tripod, trike, or prism. You certainly do not want to make that mistake with the Trinity. Your Bible makes more than a hundred references to the Holy Spirit. Jesus says more about the Holy Spirit than He does about the church, marriage, finances, and the future.

In fact, on the day of His ascension, as He prepared His followers to face the future without Him, He made this great and precious promise in Acts 1:8 (NIV):

"You will receive power when the Holy Spirit comes on you."

GOD'S PROMISE:

Your night will come to an end; there will be joy in the morning.

> ### MY PROMISE:
>
> *I will praise God before my prayer is answered.*

The disciples wanted Jesus to stay with them after His resurrection and establish His Kingdom on earth. But Jesus had different plans. Better plans. He told them in John 16:17 (NIV):

"But in fact, it is best for you that I _____, because if I do not, the _____ won't come. If I do go away, then I will send _____."

Jesus told them that it was actually *better* if He left so that He could ask the Father to send them another helper, one that would live with them and be *in* them. (See John 14:16–17.)

Just like an extra push to get you to the top of a hill, the Holy Spirit promises to do this for believers. After Jesus ascended into heaven, the Holy Spirit became the primary agent of the Trinity on earth. He will complete what was begun by the Father and the Son. Though all three expressions of the Godhead are active, the Spirit is taking the lead in this, the final age. The Spirit promises to give us a push. P-U-S-H.

- Power

- Unity

- Supervision

- Holiness

Need a push?

He promises power to the saint. He is the animating force behind creation. The Bible says:

If it were his intention and he withdrew his _____, all humanity would perish together and mankind would _____ _____. (Job 34:14–15 NIV).

The Spirit of God is a life-giving force to creation and, more significantly, a midwife of new birth for the believer. Jesus told Nicodemus: No one can enter the kingdom of God unless they are born of water and the Spirit. Flesh gives birth to flesh, but the Spirit gives birth to spirit. (See John 3:5–6.)

The Holy Spirit enters the believer upon confession of faith. From that point forward, the Christian has access to the very power and personality of God. As the Spirit has His way in the life of the believer, a transformation occurs. He or she begins to think like God thinks, love like God loves, and see like God sees. They minister in power, and pray in power, and walk in power.

When the disciples were gathered all together in the upper room, the Holy Spirit showed up on the scene. And what an entrance! The disciples described it as a mighty wind and fire. The Spirit of God promised to be with them and in them. The Holy Spirit baptized the early believers in power and promises to do the same for all who follow.

For you and me.

In Galatians, we are told that the manifestation or fruit of the Spirit in a believer is "love, joy, peace, forbearance, kindness, goodness, faithfulness, gentleness and self-control" (Galatians 5:22).

These attributes appear in the life of the saint in the same way an apple appears on the branch of an apple tree. Fruit happens as a result of relationship. Sever the branch from the tree and forget the fruit. Yet, if the branch is secure to the trunk, then the nutrients flow and the fruit happens.

So it is with the fruit of the Holy Spirit. As our relationship with God is secured and unmarred by rebellion, sin, or stubborn behavior—we can expect a harvest of fruit. We needn't force it. But we can expect it. It is simply our job to stay connected. At the right time, we will feel the power of the Spirit helping us.

We will also enjoy some gifts of the Spirit. After providing a list of possible gifts, the apostle Paul clarifies:

All these are _____ of one and the same _____, and he distributes them to each one, just as he determines (1 Corinthians 12:11 NIV).

This is so that we can be empowered for the work of the ministry. The first time the disciples experienced the Holy Spirit was when Jesus had been baptized. Scripture says that the Holy Spirit descended upon Jesus as a dove. God confirmed Him as His Son, and the Holy Spirit empowered Him for the work.

The Holy Spirit equips us as well. He knows each saint and knows the needs of each church. He distributes gifts according to what the church will need in a particular region and generation. And, the result is unity.

The Holy Spirit of God is the mother hen with her extended wing, urging the church to gather together in safety. We are told to:

Make every effort to keep the _____ through the bond of peace (Ephesians 4:3 NIV).

Saints are never told to create unity, but rather to keep the unity that the Spirit provides. Harmony is always an option because the Spirit is always present.

Gone is the excuse: "I just cannot work alongside so-and-so." Or, "So-and-so does not think like me so I cannot be on his team." Maybe you cannot, but the Spirit within you can. This unity is possible regardless of gender, nationality, or political affiliation.

Fellowship is not always easy, but *unity* is always possible. Ephesians 2:18 (NIV) tells us:

For _____ we both have access to the Father by

_____.

The Holy Spirit unifies the church. And the Holy Spirit supervises the church.

Want to hear some of His to-do list?

• Comfort the bereaved

• Guide the believer into all truth

• Reveal the things that are still to come

• Offer prayers of intercession

• Bear witness that the saint is saved

• Attest to the presence of God with signs and miracles

• Create a godlike atmosphere of truth, wisdom, and freedom

However, the list of His activities is varied, wonderful, and incomplete without this word: holiness. The Spirit of God makes us: holy.

After all, is He not the HOLY Spirit? One of His primary activities is to cleanse us from sin and to sanctify us for holy work. Paul reminds the Corinthians:

"But you were washed, you were sanctified, you were justified in the name of the Lord Jesus Christ and by the _____ _____" (1 Corinthians 6:11 NIV).

I have seen images of women washing clothes by rubbing the garments on a washboard. Perhaps the image is a good one for the work of the Holy Spirit. He rubs us until the result is spotlessness. Consequently, we can stand before the presence of God. And we are empowered for the work of the ministry.

Hear the words of Paul to Titus. The words ring true for us today:

But when the kindness and love of God our Savior appeared, _____, not because of righteous things we had done, but because _____. He saved us through the washing of rebirth and renewal by _____, whom he poured out on us generously through Jesus Christ our Savior, so that, having been justified by _____, we might become heirs having the hope of eternal life (Titus 3:4–7 NIV).

What hope this gives us! The Holy Spirit is everything to the church. He gives us power, unity, supervision, and holiness. And He will do so until the end of the age. So, for heaven's sake, "walk by the Spirit."

You can place your heart on the promise that "You will receive power when the Holy Spirit comes on you." So let's make this promise back:

I will seek to sense, see, and hear the Holy Spirit.

QUESTIONS FOR REFLECTION:

1. God as the Father. Jesus as the Son. We have human examples to help us understand these divine relationships. How would you describe the Holy Spirit using human examples?

_____

_____

_____

_____

_____

2. What are some of the scriptural roles of the Holy Spirit?

_____

_____

_____

_____

_____

3. How can you hear the Holy Spirit speak to you on a daily basis?

_____

_____

_____

_____

_____

PRAYING THE PROMISE:

Holy Spirit, You are, in very nature, God Himself.
You dwell in me and reach into parts of my soul that even I cannot reach.
You comfort me. You counsel me. You cleanse me.
By Your grace and mercy, cultivate the soil of my heart,
so that Your fruit can be produced in my life.
Amen.

Chapter Twenty-Four:

God Will Build His Church

No one told me they were going to take her away. Denalyn and I enjoyed the rehearsal dinner for our wedding. We talked with family and friends; retold stories of how we met, fell in love and got engaged; and then they took her away. Her loved ones whisked away my soon-to-be bride with the assurance, "We will have her ready for tomorrow's wedding."

Jesus knows the feeling. Did you know that the church is called the bride of Christ? Like a groom waiting in anticipation to take his bride, this picture helps us understand the anticipation of the day when Christ will come back for the church. We are being prepared for a great wedding, an eternal union with the groom.

Revelation 19:7 (NIV) gives us a quick glimpse into the time of this reunion of Christ and His church: **Let us be glad and rejoice, and let us give honor to him. For the time has come for the** _____ **of the Lamb, and** _____ **has prepared herself.**

Some years ago, I came up with a sermon illustration that fell flat. We were studying the topic of this chapter, the Church. I pointed out that the Bible calls the Church the "Bride of Christ." Upon that cue, a bride appeared at the top of the center aisle of the sanctuary. What better way to conclude the sermon, I thought, than to invite the bride of Christ to walk down the center aisle. We recruited a volunteer, dressed her in a wedding gown and veil: a veil which covered her face. At the appropriate time, I signaled for the music to start and the bride to begin her walk.

She did…she walked into the back pew. I do not know how I expected her to do anything else; the veil covered her face. She gathered herself and set out again, only to walk into another pew. She could not stay on the path. She pinballed her way into several pews before someone mercifully stepped out to guide her down the aisle.

The image is apt. We, too, sway from side to side. We, too, struggle to find our way as the Bride of Christ. Yet God has sent His Spirit to accompany us. He knows a veil blocks our vision. He knows we trip and fall. We are not as faithful as we should be at times. We do not always respond when He calls to spend time with us. We are often preoccupied by less important things.

But still, He calls us his own. He still calls us His bride.

And something tells me that He, like we, will cite the appearance of the bride as the highlight of the final wedding.

Between now and then, however, preparation needs to happen. A wedding does not come together without preparation. The invitations sent, the ceremony planned, the individual lives of the couple being lined up as one. Christ promises that the preparation for that day will take place. In fact, He takes responsibility for the development of His Church.

When God builds something, He builds it to last. In Matthew 16:18, He promises:

"I will build my _____, and all the powers of hell will not

_____" (NIV).

Jesus began building His Church during His time of ministry on earth. And it started with His disciples.

There was not a theologian among them. Not a single rabbi, scribe, or priest. Not a scholar in the bunch. No one had studied abroad or traveled the world. Most of them were low-class and blue-collared. More backwoods than uptown; blue-collar than blue blood. Common people of common stock. With common weaknesses. They could be petty and snarky. Grumpy, even. They argued with each other. They even argued with Jesus.

They told Him what He couldn't do and what He should. They snored when they should have prayed. They ran when they should have stayed. For forerunners of faith, they certainly had their share of doubts.

When Jesus invited them to walk on water, only one got out of the boat. When He fell asleep in the storm, they accused Him of falling asleep on the job. When He told them to feed the crowds, they thought He was out of his mind. When He promised to come back from the dead, they dismissed the thought.

None of them, not one of them, expected Him to do so. On five different occasions He assured them that He would vacate the grave. But were they looking for Him on Easter morning? Hardly. They hid behind locked doors. Even after His resurrection, after nearly six weeks of watching a was-dead man eat, walk, and breathe some of the disciples still doubted. Stunning.

The first followers of Jesus. Thick-headed and slow to believe. Saints? Scholars? Sages?

Hardly. We've turned them into stained-glass icons. We've named churches, colleges, and cathedrals after them. They would have laughed at such a thought. They weren't that special, which makes the promise of Jesus even more so.

GOD'S PROMISE:

My Church is unshakable.

MY PROMISE:

I will align myself with God's forever family.

The city of Caesarea Philippi sat squarely on the boundary between Israel and the Gentile world. It attracted caravans and pilgrims from as far south as Ethiopia and north as Ephesus and Asia Minor. As much as any city in ancient Palestine, this was a melting pot of people. Part Las Vegas, part Times Square, part Vatican City. It was in the maelstrom of culture that Jesus asked Peter and His other disciples: "Who do you say that I am?"

Jesus did not pose this question in Galilee, where He was applauded and followed by crowds.

Nor in Capernaum where He was the most popular rabbi. This was not Cana where Jesus rescued the wineless wedding or Jericho where Jesus enjoyed a parade. This was cosmopolitan Caesarea Philippi. Against the back-drop of this city, He asked.

"Who do you say that I am?"

It was Peter's turn to answer. Peter was always a wild card. Full of passion and zeal. He could remember the first time he had encountered Jesus. After a long hot day of fishing without a catch he was ready to throw in the towel… or the net in his case. But this man Jesus had insisted that he try one more time. Peter had never seen such a catch! More than his nets could bring in. But it was what Jesus said after that moment that changed his life. "From now on, Peter, you'll be fishing for people."

Jesus invited. Peter accepted. And what an adventure it was! What amazing things he saw! The lame walked. The blind could see. The five thousand fed. The dead raised to life. The storms silenced. The water become as pavement beneath his feet—well, at least for a moment or two. He was still mad at himself for taking his eyes of Jesus and looking at the waves.

After what might have been a long silence, he gave his answer: "You are the Christ, the Son of the living God" (Matthew 16:16).

Jesus said:

"_____ has not revealed this to you, but _____ who is in heaven" (Matthew 16:17 NIV).

Peter did not arrive at this conviction by human logic, open-mindedness, or spiritual discernment. He reached this pinnacle because God carried him to it. God deposited a seed of faith and one seed was all Jesus needed to inaugurate the most ambitious mission of history: the Church. Everything in Jesus' ministry had led up to this point. The Virgin Birth. The Nazarene upbringing. Introduced by John the Baptist. Baptized in the Jordan. Water-walking and cadaver-calling. Up until this point, Christ had done much. And now we know why.

The Carpenter had another project on the table. The same man who formed tables, chairs, and oxcarts in Nazareth unveiled a blueprint in Philippi. He told Peter:

"On this Rock I will build my church, and all the powers of hell will not conquer it" (Matthew 16:18 NLT).

Upon this unshakable belief that Jesus was the Son of God, the hope of the Church would be built.

"I will build my Church."

The operative word is "build." To build is to shape, form, nail, and create. Builders build.

Jesus is "building" His church. Selecting stones. He is lifting you from your pile and me from mine and cementing us together. He is building His Church.

"*I* will build…" He explained. Jesus did not delegate this task. You do not build the Church, nor do I. We may push the wheelbarrow or sweep the floor, but Jesus and Jesus alone is the Master craftsman. Christ is in charge. And Christ does not fail.

"I *will* build…" Not, "I might build…" or "I am hoping to build…" Or "If I can get all the problems solved I will build…" No. Jesus will complete this project. Once He begins a work, He finishes it.

He will build His *Church.* This is the first time the word appears in the Bible. Ecclesia. It means the called-out ones. The assembled. The gathered.

Satan will try to defeat us. He will divide us for a time. He will sidetrack us for a generation or ten. He will pull us down into his dark cavern for decades at a time, but he will not prevail. But the Church of Jesus Christ, built on the person of Jesus, will. God's plan has always been to build His Church; to employ common people in His uncommon cause.

People. Common people. Tax-collecting, fish-catching, bread-baking, path-walking people.

People just like you and me. We are the hands and feet of Jesus. We are His ambassadors. We are His answer to the hungry and His response to the discouraged.

He could have used angels. He could have created a super-human species of evangelistic robots. He could have deputized lions and cheetahs and eagles. But He chose us.

And therein lies the rub. The Church, like people, is imperfect.

I know this well. I am in my fourth decade of ministry. I have seen a church used for self-promotion, profiteering, and politics. I have seen church members argue, bicker, and divide. I can relate to the story of the man who told his wife: "Today is Sunday and I am not going to church. I have had enough of those people."

His wife answered, "There are two reasons you have to go. One, God commands us to love the Church. Two, you are the pastor."

Let's not give up. Under his care, impetuous Peters will become preachers. Sons of Thunder will evolve into Apostles of Hope. Thomases will step out of the shadow of doubts and Mary Magdalenes will find grace for their past. Jesus will build His church.

Align your life with this promise.

When you said yes to Christ, you said yes to His Church. Jesus did not add an invitation to His declaration to Peter. "I will build my Church. Who wants to join?" He did not give us the choice because He knew we might refuse it. We are one messy lot. Every imaginable hang-up, heartbreak, and headache. We come from all tax-brackets, tribes, latitudes, and attitudes. We disagree on politics, presidents, and pre-millennialism. Yet, for all that separates us, there is one truth that unites us.

We believe that Jesus Christ is the Son of God.

And upon that foundation, Jesus is building a movement.

The bride is being prepared. She may need some work. She may have a blemish or two. But do not doubt for a moment the love of the groom for the bride.

Hold this promise close to your heart:

"I will build my church, and all the powers of hell will not conquer it."

You are the church. So make this your own promise:

I will align myself with God's forever family.

QUESTIONS FOR REFLECTION:

1. What is the difference between "a church" and "the Church"?

_____

_____

_____

_____

_____

2. Why do you suppose Jesus decided to use broken and flawed men and women to form His Church?

_____

_____

_____

_____

_____

3. Why is it important for you to be committed to a community of fellow believers? What are the benefits for your spiritual growth?

_____

_____

_____

_____

_____

PRAYING THE PROMISE:

Jesus, you are the Cornerstone of the Church.
Our foundation is based on You and Your great promises.
And yet we—the stones
You have chosen to construct the Church—are rough and unpolished.
Often we do not fit well together.
We pray that Your Holy Spirit would shape us and form us,
so that we fit well together.
Unify Your Church in love that we may be a light to the world.
Amen.

Chapter Twenty-Five:

God Will Meet All Your Needs

If ever there were an uninvited guest at our life's party, it would be Worry. It does not have a single positive thing to offer anyone. And yet it quietly unlocks the door to our hearts and minds and slips in unannounced. Then it stealthily settles into a place of comfort and makes plans to stay for the long haul.

When politely asked to leave, it nonchalantly declines. Then it resumes its relentless routine of casting a dark shadow of fear in the heart and light-blocking shade on our outlook. Under the weight of worry's spell, we feel and see things that have not even happened yet and maybe never will.

You can see it happening all around you if look close enough.

A traveler stands in the airport security line and removes her bracelet. She's already placed her shoes in a rubberized bin, liquids in the plastic bag, and removed the boarding pass from her purse. She wonders about the fungus on the floor. Will she miss her flight? Will the flight make it on time? Will it make it at all? She hates the thought, but permits it anyway. Any day now her luck is going to run out!

Meanwhile, there is a fellow sitting on the back row of the English as a Second Language class.

He would prefer the front row, but by the time he caught the city bus and endured the evening traffic, the best seats were taken. His hands still smell of diner dishwater where Worry worked since 6:00 a.m. Within twelve hours he'll be at the sink again, but for now he does his best to make sense of verbs, adverbs, and nouns. Everyone else seems to get it. He does not. He never diagrammed a sentence in Spanish, how will he ever do it in English? Yet, with no English, how will he ever do more than wash plates? Worry has more questions than answers, work than energy, and thinks often about giving up.

I know how those two feel. Worry has woven its way into my home, as well. I recently awoke at 4:30 a.m., struggling with a message. It needed to be finished by 5:00 p.m. I pulled the pillow over my head and tried in vain to return to the blissful netherworld of sleep that knows nothing of deadlines or completion dates. But it was too late. The starter's pistol had fired. An Olympic squad of synapses was racing in my brain, stirring a wake of adrenaline. So, Worry climbed out of bed, dressed, and slipped out of the house into the silent streets and drove to the office. I grumbled, first about the crowded calendar, next about my poor time management. Worry unlocked the door, turned on the computer, and stared at the passage on the monitor.

But then I smiled. There on the screen was some very clear direction. Matthew 6:25 (NIV) yielded some precious words that Jesus spoke about worrying:

"So I tell you, _____ about everyday life—whether you have enough…"

Shortfalls and depletions inhabit our trails. Not enough time, luck, wisdom, intelligence. We are running out of everything, it seems, and so we worry. But worry does not work.

A better way is right in front of us. The passage in Matthew continues:

"Look at the birds. They do not need to plant or harvest or put food in barns because your _____ feeds them. And you are far more valuable to him than they are. Can all your worries _____ to your life? Of course not" (Matthew 6:26–27 NIV).

Fret won't fill a bird's belly with food or a flower's petal with color. Birds and flowers seem to get along just fine, and they do not take antacids. What is more, you can dedicate a decade of anxious thoughts to the brevity of life and not extend it by one minute. Worry accomplishes nothing.

Jesus does not condemn legitimate concern for responsibility, but rather the continuous mindset that dismisses God's presence. Destructive anxiety subtracts God from the future, faces uncertainties with no faith, tallies up the challenges of the day without entering God into the equation. Worry is the dark room where negatives become glossy prints.

Ever heard the song, "Don't Worry, Be Happy"? Well, did you know it is actually possible? There is a hope-filled promise in Philippians 4:19 that says: *God will meet all your needs.*

My friend saw an example of perpetual uneasiness in his six-year-old daughter. In her hurry to dress for school, she tied her shoelaces in a knot. She plopped down at the base of the stairs and fixated her thoughts on the tangled mess. The school bus was coming and the minutes were ticking, and she gave no thought to the fact that her father was standing nearby, willing to help upon request. Her little hands began to shake and tears began to drop. Finally, in an expression of total frustration, she dropped her forehead to her knees and sobbed.

That's a child-sized portrait of destructive worry. A knot-fixation to the point of anger and exasperation, oblivious to the presence of our Father, who stands nearby. My friend finally took it upon himself to come to his daughter's aid.

Why did she not request her father's help to start with? We could ask the same of ourselves. Next time you are quaking from anxiety, take a look at this unshakable promise found in Philippians 4:19: God will meet all your needs.

Pray, first. Do not pace up and down the floors of the waiting room—pray for a successful surgery. Do not bemoan the collapse of an investment—ask God to help you. Do not join the chorus of coworkers who complain about your boss—invite them to bow their heads with you and pray for him. Inoculate yourself inwardly to face your fears outwardly with prayer.

Imitate the mother of Jesus at the wedding in Cana. The reception was out of wine, a huge social no-no in the days of Jesus. Mary could have blamed the host for poor planning, or the guests for overdrinking, but she did not catastrophize. No therapy sessions or counseling. Instead, she presented the problem to Jesus. And He turned the water to wine. Problem solved.

When you have a problem, what is your first response? Panic? Outcry? Worry? Who has got time for that? Quickly assess the problem, take it to Jesus, and let Him do His work!

Become a worry slapper. Treat frets like mosquitoes. Do you procrastinate when a blood-sucking bug lands on your skin, thinking, "I will take care of it in a moment." Of course you do not! You give the critter the slap it deserves. Be equally decisive with anxiety. The moment a concern surfaces, deal with it. Do not dwell on it. Head worries off before they get the best of you. Do not waste an hour wondering what your boss thinks, ask her. Before you diagnose that mole as cancer, have it examined. Instead of assuming you'll never get out of debt, consult an expert. Be a doer, not a stewer.

Where can you find the strength to kick worry out the door and make room for the peace that's promised? By claiming and trusting in the precious promise of Philippians 4:19: "God will meet all your needs." And that means *all of them.*

GOD'S PROMISE:

I will meet all of your needs.

MY PROMISE:

I will trust God to meet my needs.

If ever there were a place where worrying might not just be prevalent, but even overpowering, it would probably be prison. Imagine what goes through the mind of a man in chains pondering his fate. Will he be subjected to torture? Will he ever see his wife and children again? Will he become sick and waste away from malnutrition? Will he be forgotten and left here to die? Or be sentenced to death in a public display to teach others a lesson? So many dark thoughts could enter into an incarcerated man's heart.

But not if that man was Paul. He chose another path. Paul was impoverished. The very reason we have the letter called Philippians is because a church took pity on his poverty. He had no money. But he had joy in his heart. It may have been all he had, but it was enough.

He had no health. His tired body carried the marks of whippings, shipwrecks, and disease. He spoke of a thorn in the flesh and complained of a frailty of his eyes. His money was gone, his health was failing.

And, what is worse, his life work was in jeopardy. The Galatians were defecting. The Corinthian church was squabbling. The Ephesian church was struggling. The Romans needed encouraging. It was a tough time for Paul. Purse empty. Health fleeting. Churches battling. And in the midst of it all, he ended up in jail. What a lousy time to be arrested! The old apostle did not even have good timing.

The wrap of old age hangs from his shoulders. His chin sags like worn cloth and the Roman chain rests at his feet like a tired dog. Paul is at the end of the line, a long line.

But give him half a chance and he will tell you the story of stories. He will tilt his large head to the side and smile a wry smile. He'll speak of the light that left him blind and the voice that left him speechless.

"Saul, Saul," Jesus had spoken.

Just as Abraham was called to walk by faith, just as Moses was called to deliver the slaves, now Saul was called to do both. And about the same time Nero was born in Rome, Saul became Paul and was born again in Damascus. For the next three decades, neither Paul nor the world would be the same.

Tireless. Focused. Unfailingly faithful. He crisscrossed the Eastern world stitching tents, preaching Christ, and planting churches. He was angular, forceful, brilliant, and unmovable. And because he wouldn't budge, the church feared him before they loved him and he slept in more jails than hotels. But that was okay with Paul. Suffering was tolerable because he had the one thing that mattered.

He had the Lord.

He, the sinner, had met Christ, the Savior, and the sinner was never to be silenced. Put him in a synagogue and he would preach. Put him in a boat and he would witness. Put him in jail and he would write.

Here is a curious question. Had you been a Roman citizen in 61 or 62 AD and someone gave you the choice, would you rather be Emperor Nero or Apostle Paul? Lounging in the palace or locked away in prison? Which would you have chosen? Ask Paul the question and he would be quick to answer. *My purse may be empty, but my Father's is always full.*

Paul embraced the very words he wrote in Philippians 4:19:

My God will meet _____ your needs according to the _____ of his glory in Christ Jesus.

Voilà! That's the promise. That was the discovery of Paul. That is the hope of the believer. God is in charge of our lives. No matter how dire our circumstances might appear, He will give you everything you need, even from within a prison cell.

For most of us, our prisons are not made of walls. We are imprisoned by the past, by our fears, by our guilt, by our anger, by our hurts. We are imprisoned by a thousand and one invisible stones stacked cruelly upon each other.

But we, like Paul, can plant a garden of peace in our prison of problems. You needn't search far to see the good that Paul did. Not a day passes that thousands are not instructed and inspired by the life of Paul. His is one of the most enduring names.

If you had the choice, if you were offered a palace with no Christ or a prison with Christ, which would you choose?

Some of you are like Paul. So much has been taken over the years. Health, friends, family, future. Some of you are like Paul in prison. Only your prison is not made of walls, it is made of circumstances. But look at you. There is still a twinkle in your eye and song on your lips. You have learned well. Like Paul, you too have maintained a joyful heart. Rather than being paralyzed with worry of what may come, you are moving forward in faith with your confidence in Christ.

Others of us could learn a little more. Instead of focusing on what is wrong in our lives, we could turn our eyes to what is right. Rather than using our voice to complain we could use it to sing. And rather than living in fear we could live in faith.

We needn't give any room in our lives to worry. We have a promise that God will meet all of our needs. And with that promise our hearts can be filled with joy and thankfulness. It is not a question of whether He'll do it. It is simply a question of whether we will choose to believe it, and act accordingly. No matter what chains are holding you back today, or what prison bars are blocking your progress and stealing away your freedom, I encourage you to remember God's promise...and then make it your own:

"I will trust God to meet my needs."

QUESTIONS FOR REFLECTION:

1. What are your three biggest needs right now?

_____

_____

_____

_____

_____

2. What are the obstacles you face in having your needs met?

_____

_____

_____

_____

_____

3. Are you ready to entrust your needs to the One who said He will meet all of your needs? What, if anything, is holding you back?

_____

_____

_____

_____

_____

PRAYING THE PROMISE:

Jesus, what an incredible promise You have given to me—
that You will meet ALL of my needs through Your riches.
When fear and doubt creep into my mind,
make me like the man in the Gospels who cried,
"I believe, but please help my unbelief."
Help me to turn my eyes from my needs to Your mercy
and Your riches in grace.
Amen.

Chapter Twenty-Six:

God Has Set a Day of Judgment

In the predawn hours of December 14, 2012, Daniel Barden awoke early and reveled in the sight of the sunrise. Through a silhouette of bare trees, the dark sky outside their Newtown, Connecticut, home turned red-orange. Christmas tree lights, reflected on the window, dotted the sunrise.

"Isn't that beautiful?" seven-year-old Daniel asked his father, who captured the moment in a photo before walking his son to the school bus.

Daniel was one of twenty children and six adults shot to death at Sandy Hook Elementary School later that morning.

Mark, Daniel's father, has reflected on that final morning more times than he can count. He remembers how Daniel took a moment to hug his sister Natalie and see her off to the school bus. They played "Jingle Bells" on the piano. Later Daniel ran down the stairs, his toothbrush still in his mouth, to hug and kiss his mother before she left for work.

On most mornings, when Mark Barden walked Daniel to the school bus, his son insisted on a quick game of tag.

"Do we have to play tag today?" Mark asked Daniel that morning. "Can we just hold hands today?" So they did. They just held hands.

David had no way of knowing the rage that was about to erupt. A deranged gunman was lying in wait for the opportunity to slaughter innocent people. Sandy Hook was not the first massacre in American history. But it seemed the cruelest. These weren't adults, they were children. This was not a war, it was a quiet neighborhood. These weren't gangsters, they were elementary aged kids at an elementary school on a holiday morning. The kids did not deserve death. Their parents do not deserve such grief. And we've received an all too common reminder: life is not fair.

When did you learn those words? *It is not fair.* What deed exposed you to the imbalanced scales of life? Did a car wreck leave your mother a widow? Did a disease leave your body disfigured? Did friends forget you, a teacher ignore you, an adult abuse you? When did you discover the injustice of life? When did you first pray the prayer of the prophet Jeremiah? *Why does the way of the wicked prosper?* (See Jeremiah 12:1.)

There are so many questions that are easy to ask and hard to answer. Why do drug peddlers get rich? Sex-offenders get off? Charlatans get elected? Murderers get out? Cheaters get by? Scoundrels get in? How long will injustice flourish?

God's answer is direct: not long.

Take confidence in knowing that justice will be served. Maybe not in our preferred time, but in God's perfect time. He is not sitting idly by. He is not twiddling His thumbs. Every flip of the calendar brings us closer to the day in which He will judge all evil.

The apostle Paul assures us in the Book of Acts that:

God has set a day when he will _____ the world (Acts 17:31 NIV).

To "set" means to "single out." A Judgment Day has been chosen. The hour is marked and moment reserved. Judgment is not a possibility, but a stark reality.

"Judgment Day" is an unpopular term. We dislike the image of a great hour of reckoning, which is ironic. We disdain judgment but we value justice, yet the second is impossible without the first. One cannot have justice without judgment. For that reason the judgment seat shares equal status with the king's throne as the two symbols of the Great Day.

Matthew 25:31 (NIV) tells that on the day Jesus returns:

...he will _____ on his glorious _____.

All people of all nations will bow low before His authority. Every person will acknowledge the King and His one-king kingdom.

Paul tell us in 2 Corinthians 5:10, "We must all appear before the judgment seat of Christ, so that each of us may receive what is due us for the things done while in the body, whether good or bad."

Justice will prevail.

This promise may not matter to you. For some people, life feels fair and just. If that describes you, count your blessings. There are others, however, who fight a daily battle with anger. They've been robbed; evil people have pilfered days with their loved ones, disease has sapped health from their body. They believe that justice must be served.

I am one of these people. My brother was robbed. Alcoholism heisted the joy out of his life. For two-thirds of his fifty-seven years, he battled the bottle. It cost him his family, finances, and friends. He was not innocent, I get that. He bought the liquor and made the choices. Yet, I am convinced that Satan assigned a special goon squad to tempt him. When they found his weakness, they refused to let up. They took him to the mat and pounded the self-control out of him.

I am ready to see Satan pay for his crimes against my brother. I am looking forward to that moment when I stand next to Dee our bodies redeemed and souls secure. Together we will see the devil bound and chained and cast into a lake of fire. At that point we will begin to reclaim what the devil took.

Can I encourage you to place all the injustices of life before Christ?

Follow the examples of the women of the Dinka village in Sudan.

Government-backed soldiers ravaged their settlement, butchering and brutalizing more than a hundred people. Muslim fundamentalists captured the strong, abandoned the weak, burned huts, and razed crops. The horror, however, gave birth to hope. A remnant of survivors, wives, and mothers of the murdered and missing gathered sticks and tied them together in the form of small crosses.

Before they buried the bodies and mourned their losses, they pressed the crosses into the ground. Not as memorials to their grief, but as declarations of their hope. They were Jesus-followers. The crossed sticks expressed their living faith in a loving God who could and *will* make sense of such tragedy.

Do the same with your tragedies. Place them in the shadow of the cross and be reminded: God understands injustice. He will right all wrongs and heal all wounds. He has prepared a place where life will be finally and forever…just.

GOD'S PROMISE:

I have set a day when I will judge the world.

MY PROMISE:

I will respect God's justice and delight in God's grace.

The apostle Paul is lauded for his ability to be content in all circumstances. I think it is because he had the ability to look beyond the present and focus on the future. While he might be poor, the riches of heaven awaited him. While he might be captive in a dungy prison cell, he would soon be free walking the glorious streets of heaven. Paul was sure of his future, and that changed his perspective on the present.

He had faith in God. And that in God's perfect time, justice would be served. The Greek word for judgment seat is *bema*. The term denotes a court in session, a place where the judge is present and the verdicts declared. From His throne Jesus will forever balance the scales of fairness. He will do so through three declarations:

First, He will publicly pardon His people.

When Paul said "we must all appear before the judgment seat of Christ," he meant everyone. "All" includes all humanity. Paul did not exclude his name from this list nor can we.

We may want to. Especially when we consider that, according to Romans 2:16, this will be "the day when God judges people's secrets through Jesus Christ." I do not want you to hear my secret thoughts. I do not want my viewers to know the sermons I dreaded or conversations I avoided. Why will Christ expose every deed of the Christian heart? For the sake of justice. He must declare each sin forgiven.

God filters His verdict through Jesus. Believers won't stand before the bench alone. Jesus will be at our side. As the sin is disclosed, so is the forgiveness.

When a voice says, "Max lied to his teacher," Jesus' voice will say, "I took his punishment." When a voice says, "Max stretched the truth," Jesus' voice will say, "I died for that sin."

When a voice says, "Max complained again," Jesus' voice will say, "I know. I have forgiven him." On and on the reading will go until every sin of every believer is proclaimed and pardoned.

God's justice demands a detailed accounting. He will not permit the hint of injustice in His new kingdom. Every citizen will know that every sin has been surfaced and pardoned. Heaven cannot be heaven with secrets or buried pasts.

But you won't be embarrassed. To the contrary, you will be stunned. Your awe will grow as the list of forgiven sins lengthens.

The result will be a heaven draped in justice. No saint will look upon another with suspicion. No saint will look into his or her past with guilt. All will be disclosed. All will be forgiven. The public display of forgiven sins will prompt eternal gratitude to our Savior.

But wait—that's not all! There is even more good news for God's people.

The second declaration is that He will applaud the service of His servants.

Paul tells us, "He will bring to light what is hidden in darkness and will expose the motives of the heart. At that time each will receive their praise from God" (1 Corinthians 4:5 NIV).

God will walk you through your life day-by-day, moment-by-moment. As if a video replays your biography, He will issue commendation after commendation. "You gave up your seat on the bus. Well done. You greeted the new student in your class. Fine job. You forgave your brother, encouraged your neighbor… you stayed awake during Max's message, I am so proud of you."

God records and rewards your goodness. It is only fair that He does. And since He is a just God, He will declare the pardon of His people, applaud the service of His servants.

As the general places a medal on Hhis soldiers, God places a robe on his. But for those who would fight against God, the third declaration now applies:

He will honor the wishes of the wicked.

The apostle Paul wrote in Romans 1:21 and 23 that some people will stand before God who did not treat Him like God, refusing to worship Him. They traded the glory of God who holds the whole world in His hands for cheap figurines you can buy at any roadside stand. They spent a lifetime dishonoring the King and hurting His people. They mocked His name and made life miserable for their neighbors.

A just God must honor the wishes of God-rejecters.

Even our judicial system, fragile as it may be, forces no defense on the accused. The defendant is offered an advocate, but if he chooses to stand before the judge alone, the system permits it.

So does God. He offers His Son as advocate. Jesus will stand in judgment at the side of every person, except those who refuse Him. When their deeds are read, heaven's tribunal will hear nothing but silence.

"You denied My presence." Silence.

"You abused My children." Silence.

"You slandered My name." Silence.

"You ignored My Word." Silence.

"You rejected My Son." Silence.

What response can be given? What defense can be offered? God is right. God is just. No one in heaven or hell will accuse the judge of injustice when He announces, "Depart from me, you who are cursed, into the eternal fire prepared for the devil and his angels" (Matthew 25:42 NIV).

Indeed, justice will prevail.

Paul was very clear. A day is coming when scores will be settled. Let this covenant abate the anger you feel at the hurting world. Devastations have bloodied every generation. Does our globe have one square mile of unstained soil? The Hutus slaughtered 800,000 Tutsis. Hitler exterminated six million Jews and gypsies. American bombs devastated Hiroshima and Nagasaki. Japanese tortured American soldiers. Suicide bombs in Baghdad, mass murders at Sandy Hook; it is not right, it is not just, it is not fair that the evil prosper. When you wonder if the unrepentant wicked will go unpunished or injustices will go unaddressed, let this promise gratify your desire for justice. God will have the final word.

Route the tragedies of life through the justice of the future. Do not think God does not see evil or understand the inequities. He will balance His scales. He will right all wrongs and heal all wounds. He has prepared a place where life will be finally and forever fair. You can be sure of this. God gives you His promise:

For [God] has set a day when he will judge the world.

Now make your own promise.

I will respect God's justice and delight in God's grace.

QUESTIONS FOR REFLECTION:

1. In many circles, it is unpopular to talk about God's judgment. Why do you think that is?

_____

_____

_____

_____

_____

2. What is the purpose of God's judgment? (Hint: Review the three declarations.)

_____

_____

_____

_____

3. We just read that "God will have the final word." What will His final word be for you?

_____

_____

_____

_____

Praying the Promise:

God, I know You are just and righteous.
One day stand I will stand before You in judgment,
and apart from Your grace,
I deserve eternal punishment.
Yet You have offered me forgiveness by the cross of Christ.
Grace—a gift I cannot earn—is there for me to receive from You.
Help me to speak the truth about Your Day of Judgment in love
and to embrace the grace that is from You.
Amen.

CHAPTER TWENTY-SEVEN:

GOD WILL MAKE EVERYTHING NEW

My friend Dan is an avid runner. We used to log miles together, but then I got older and he got stronger and that is a topic for a book on staying healthy. He went on to complete an Ironman Triathlon at Lake Placid, New York. Of all the Ironman events around the world, this one stands out for its community participation. The final mile of the race is run on the track of the high school stadium. The local residents pack the bleachers for the singular purpose of cheering on the finishers. They arrive in early afternoon to celebrate the winner and linger into the night to wait for the stragglers. Many of the runners do not reach the stadium until well after the sun has set.

Dan was one of these. He had been swimming, biking, and running since 8:00 a.m. His legs were cramping and feet were sore. Everything inside him wanted to quit. But then he heard the roar. Still miles from the stadium, he heard the cheers of the assembled crowd.

He quickened his pace. He could see the stadium lights in the distance. Over the PA system he heard: "And from San Antonio, Texas, Dan Smith!"

The place erupted! People he would never know were calling his name. Little kids were chanting, "Dan! Dan! Dan!" Gone was the pain. Forgotten was the weariness. He was surrounded by a huge crowd of witnesses.

So are you. Listen carefully, the passage compels, and you will hear a multitude of God's children urging you on. Noah is among them. So is Mary, the mother of Jesus. Do you hear the support of the first-century martyrs? What about the Chinese house church leaders or the eighteenth-century missionaries to Africa? Some of us have mom and dad, brother or sister—even a child—in the stands. They are part of the great cloud of witnesses.

That's also why, when these verses are understood, we celebrate.

What verses are we talking about?

Hebrews 11 says:

These were all commended for their _____, yet none of them received what had been _____, since God had planned something better for us so that only together with us would they be _____. Therefore, since we are surrounded by such a _____ _____, let us throw off everything that hinders and the sin that so easily entangles. And let us _____ _____ the race marked out for us (Hebrews 11:39–40; 12:1 NIV).

These verses are the exclamation point on one of the greatest chapters in the entire Bible. The writer of Hebrews gives us courage for the future by examining the heroes of the past. He has just escorted us through the Faith Hall of Fame.

By _____Abel brought God a better offering… (vs. 4).

By_____ Noah…built an ark… (vs. 7).

By _____ Abraham…obeyed… (vs. 8).

These were all commended for _____, yet none of them received what had been promised (Hebrews 11:39).

We expect the next verse to tell us, "They have now." We anticipate the next words of the writer to be: "In their new heavenly home, they are completely rewarded, having received in full the blessing for which they lived." But such are not the words. The writer surprises, even stuns us, by describing the someday oneness of heaven. Another version puts it this way, "Not one of these people, even though their lives of faith were exemplary, got their hands on what was promised. God had a better plan for us" (MSG).

Press the pause button on that passage. Who is the "us" in that passage? That's you and me. We are a part of the blessing of the saints. One element of their reward is "us." How could this be? How might you and I enhance the heavenly reward of Abraham, Moses, and Sara? The next verse says: "God had a better plan for us: that their faith and our faith would come together to make one completed whole, their lives of faith not complete without ours" (Hebrews 11:40 MSG).

These words teach a remarkable truth. Heaven's saints are waiting on us to show up. Heaven won't be heaven until all God's children are home.

If you have ever been a part of a family holiday celebration, you know exactly what this means.

I am the youngest of four children. By the time I was old enough to enjoy Christmas, my two older sisters had husbands and homes of their own. For me, the big moment of the holidays was less the coming of Santa and more the coming of my sisters. The sound of the car in the driveway and the voices in the doorway were great sounds. *We are all back together again!* That's the way heaven will be.

That's the way it was meant to be. We have accepted the idea that death is just a natural part of life, but it is not. Birth is. Breathing is. Belly laughs, big hugs, and bedtime kisses are. But death? Death stinks. It is hard to fathom. One reason we say so little at funerals is because we do not know what to say. Death stuns and silences us. It does not seem to fit. Why does God give us a fishing buddy and then take him? A child, and then take her? Why does God fashion and present to you the greatest husband in history if you cannot be together forever?

Death does not seem right. Indeed, it is not. It is wrong. Death intruded into the Garden of Eden as a consequence of the curse. God's original plan included no final day, breath, or heartbeats. That's why, when they come, we hurt.

But one day, we will enter that stadium and the crowd will cheer and those who have gone before us will welcome us home. All of heaven is in anticipation of that day. As wonderful as heaven is, it won't be complete until all of its children are home. And what a home it will be! Not some overrun, overpopulated relocation. No, God is preparing something new and wonderful for us.

GOD'S PROMISE:

I am making everything new!

MY PROMISE:

I will fix my eyes on things above.

After Jesus returned to heaven, the disciples did not shy away from His commission to them to go into all the world and preach the gospel. In fact, they spread out all over the known world taking the message to those who had not yet heard. But passion comes at a price, and after years of preaching, persecution, and sacrifice, we find the disciple John banished to the island of Patmos by the Roman government. For refusing to stop witnessing about Jesus, he would live out the last years of his life on an island reserved for criminals and lunatics.

But it is here, on this island of death, that John received his greatest revelation of the life to come for Christ and the church.

He wrote:

Then I, John, saw _____, New Jerusalem, coming down out of _____, prepared as a bride adorned for her husband (Revelation 21:2 NKJV).

This passage sits like an entryway painting in John's art gallery of heaven. Having just described the new heaven and new earth, he begins with a portrait of the new city. Look how excited he is: ...*I, John, saw the holy city*....

This is the first time this beloved disciple of Jesus speaks this way. The prior chapters contain no fewer than eight "I saw" statements. I saw...

- a white horse

- an angel standing

- the beast...

- the kings of the earth

- an angel coming down

But when John sees the New Jerusalem, he does something different. He personalizes the moment. "I, John, saw the holy city, New Jerusalem..." —as if John cannot believe he is the one to witness the metropolis. He's an archaeologist unearthing the Rosetta Stone, a violinist locating the first ever Stradivarius. John beholds the crown jewel of heaven: the New Jerusalem.

Why should a New Jerusalem interest us? John replies with a flurry of adjectives and metaphors that result in two explanations.

First, God has space for us.

John writes:

The angel who talked to me held in his hand a gold measuring stick to measure the city, its gates, and its wall. When he measured it, he found it was a square, as _____. In fact, its length and width and height were _____. Then he measured the walls and found them to be_____. (Revelation 21:15-17 NLT).

So, dismiss any thought of congestion in this city. John lets us know that the size of the New Jerusalem stretches the imagination: 1,400 miles in length, width, and height. Large enough to contain the land mass from the Appalachians to the West Coast. Canada to Mexico. Forty times the size of England. Ten times the size of France and larger than India. And that's just the ground floor.

The city stands as tall as it does wide. If God were to stack the city in stories as an architect would a building, the New Jerusalem would have 600,000 floors, ample space for billions of people. Ample space for you.

This life hasn't always had space for you, has it? When did you discover the congestion of this world? The school had no space for you. The team had no space for you. Your father's schedule had no space for you. Your boss just cannot find a space for you. We learn early the finite amount of resources,

Only so much time, only room for so many students, only so many seats. There is just not enough space. Consequently, we get eliminated, cut, dropped, and refused. But in heaven there is abundant space with abundant provision.

But dare we trust that God will keep His promise? Will we really experience such a place?

How can we know He won't change His mind? The answer is chiseled in the stone of New Jerusalem. God has grace for us.

John wrote about a great high wall with twelve gates and the names of the twelve tribes written on them.

Now, do not miss this message. Who are these twelve sons of Israel whose names we see on the city gates? Simeon and Levi are listed. They were the brothers who attacked a tribe and killed them all, to revenge a disgraced sister. Judah, another of the twelve, messed up and got a girl pregnant. Nine of the brothers conspired to kill another brother, Joseph, but ended up selling him into Egyptian slavery. Warring, scheming hustlers, and liars.

Sounds more like the 3:00 a.m. nightclub crowd than it does a hall of faith. Yet these are the names carved on the gate of New Jerusalem.

And dare we mention the other names on the foundations? These names make heaven's honor roll? These were the disciples who chose to leave Jesus alone to face His crucifixion while they ran and hid. Yet all of their names appear on the foundations. Matthew's does. Peter's does. Bartholomew's does. John's does.

The names of the twelve tribes and apostles; unlikely material for heaven's engravings. We engrave earth's granite with heroes and philanthropists; scholars and explorers. But what of we, who are none of the above?

"I have space and grace for you," God says. Our sins will not be remembered.

No more struggle with the earth. No more shame before God. No more tension between people. No more death. No more curse. The removal of the curse will return God's people and universe to their intended state. He will do this because of the work of Jesus Christ on the cross. Christ redeemed us from the curse of the law by becoming a curse for us. Christ endured every consequence of the curse; its shame, its humiliation, even its death. Because He did, the curse will be lifted.

Everything new. No wonder John was so enthusiastic as he transcribed what he had seen. The old will be gone. Gone with hospital waiting rooms. Gone with tear-stained divorce papers. Gone with motionless ultra-sounds. Gone with loneliness, foreclosure notices, and abuse. Gone with cancer.

Jesus says, I am making all things new.

God will lay hold of every atom, emotion, insect, animal, and galaxy. He will reclaim every diseased body and afflicted mind. To do any less would be the admission of defeat. To destroy the universe is to admit it cannot be reclaimed and renewed. To rescue and redeem it, however, is yet another display of our Maker's ultimate authority.

Romans 8:19 says: "The created world itself can hardly wait for what is coming next...." Every page and promise of the Bible invites and excites us with the lure of a new day, a new earth, and a new kingdom.

As John writes recounts in Revelation 21:5, God has promised:

"I am making everything new!"

And we can stand on this promise, with unshakable faith of what is to come, making our own promise:

"I will fix my eyes on things above."

QUESTIONS FOR REFLECTION:

1. Have you ever wanted a "do-over" in life? Is this what God means when He says He will make all things new? Why or why not?

_____

_____

_____

_____

_____

2. When does eternal life in heaven begin?

_____

_____

_____

_____

_____

3. How can you live now, in this life, in a "heavenly" way?

_____

_____

_____

_____

Praying the Promise:

Jesus, I set my heart on things above, in the heavenly places.
I look to You, for in You are hidden the riches of life.
Your plan is to make all things new,
and I believe You are redeeming people and places even now.
Keep me strong until the end that I may be found faithful
on the day You return.
Amen.

Chapter Twenty-Eight:

Build Your Life on God's Promises

When my children were young, we went on a road trip vacation. My daughters were ages five, three, and an infant. We drove from San Antonio, Texas, to Santa Fe, New Mexico. I told them about the time we would spend in the car, the mountains, the streams, and the thin cold air of the high country. They tried to imagine the trip, but still had questions, and had trouble understanding the idea of it. So they asked more questions. Will we get tired? Get lost? Will we be cold? I attempted to explain the trip to them, but they had no frame of reference. They gave me blank stares. So rather than give them information, I gave them a promise, "I will take care of you. I will get you there." They made a wonderful decision. They trusted me.

It is the same way with the promises God has made us. These promises are the stitching in the spine of the Bible. Since the beginning of time, God's relationship to man has been shaped by specific requirements and promises, unchangeable decrees that define the outflow of history.

One student of Scripture spent a year and a half attempting to tally the number of promises God made to humanity. He came up with 7,487 promises! God's promises are pine trees in the Rocky Mountains of Scripture: abundant, unbending, and perennial. Some of them are positive, the assurance of blessings. Some of them are negative, the guarantee of consequence. But all the promises are binding.

God is a promise-maker.

As God was preparing the Israelites to face a new land, He made a promise to them, that He would do wonders never before done in any nation of the world, and all would see it. (See Exodus 34:10–11.)

Notice, God did not emphasize the Israelite's strength. He emphasized His. He did not underscore their ability. He highlighted His. He equipped them for the journey by headlining His capacity to make and keep His promises.

What He says will happen. His promises are irrevocable because James 1:17 (NIV) says:

He never _____ or casts a _____ shadow.

He is unchanging. He makes no mid-course corrections. He is not victimized by moods or weather. He is faithful.

Listen to this Scripture in Hebrews. A foundational promise that all the others can stand upon. Hebrews 10:23 (NIV) says this:

God can be _____ to keep his promise.

Trusted. You can trust that if He has said it, He will follow through with it. He is strong. He does not over-promise and under-deliver. He is able to, and will, do what He promised.

Scripture says that it is impossible for God to lie. A rock cannot swim. A hippo cannot fly. A butterfly cannot eat a bowl of spaghetti. You cannot sleep on a cloud and God cannot lie. He never exaggerates, manipulates, fibs, or flatters. This verse does not say it is unlikely that God will lie or improbable that God will lie. No, the statement is clear: it is impossible! Scripture could not be more forthright. Deceit is simply not an option.

So the question then is not, Will God keep His promises? But, Will we build our lives upon them? Upon what are you building? The circumstances of life or the promises of God? We live in a day of despair. The suicide rate continues to increase. If a disease saw such a spike, we would deem it an epidemic. How do we explain the increase? We've never been more educated. We have tools of technology our parents could only dream of. We are saturated with entertainment and recreation.

Yet more people are orchestrating their own deaths than ever. How could this be?

Among the answers must be this. People are dying for *lack of hope*. Secularism sucks the hope out of society. It reduces the world to a few decades between birth and hearse. People believe that this world is as good as it gets, and let's face it, it is not that good.

But People of the Promise have an advantage. They filter life through the promises of God. When problems surface, they can be heard telling themselves, "But God said..." When struggles threaten, they can be seen flipping through Scripture, "I think God said something about this." When comforting others, they are prone to ask, "Do you know God's promise on this topic?"

Dwight Moody said it this way: "Let a man feed for a month on the promises of God, and he will not talk about how poor he is." If you would only read from Genesis to Revelation and see all the promises made by God to Abraham, to Isaac, to Jacob, to the Jews and to the Gentiles, and to all His people everywhere—if you would spend a month feeding on the precious promises of God—you wouldn't be going about complaining how poor you are. You would lift up your head and proclaim the riches of His grace, because you couldn't help doing it.

I pray that you discover the hope— *he Unshakable Hope*—that comes from building your life on the promises of God. Let's declare this together:

"I will build my life on the Promises of God."

I have many quirks, not the least of which is a shaky left thumb. For the last decade or so, it has quivered. Seriously shook. It is as if my thumb lives on a caffeine drip. Were I to drink coffee left-handed, I would slosh it everywhere. But I am not left-handed so the quiver does not bother me. I use it as a conversation starter. "Hey, can I show you my shaky thumb?"

I have grown accustomed to the localized tremor. At first, however, I was not so calm. The shaking shook me. I thought something had come unwired. Since my father had passed away from ALS, my imagination began to assume the worse. The situation was especially unnerving because left thumb follows me everywhere I go. When I comb my hair, there is old wobbly. When I putt, guess who cannot settle down. If I raise my left hand to make a point in a sermon, you might not trust what I say because of the knockety knuckle.

I set up an appointment with the neurologist and entered his office with dry mouth and dread.

He examined me. He had me walk, balance, and spin a few plates on my finger. (Just kidding. He did not make me walk.) He tapped me with the rubber hammer and asked me some questions. Then, after an interminably long time he said: "No need to worry."

"No treatment?"

"Nope?"

"No wheelchair?"

"Nope, not from what I can see."

"You sure?"

He then did something nice, he said, "I promise. Your thumb is nothing to worry about."

So, I confidently hopped down and thanked him and walked out. I felt better. At some point on the drive home, I noticed my left hand on the steering wheel. Guess what my thumb was doing. It was shaking.

For the first time I had the opportunity to look at the tremor differently. I could ponder the problem or remember the promise. I told it, "You are not getting any more of my attention." From that moment on, each time the thumb misbehaved, I thought of the promise of the doctor.

What is shaking in your world? Not likely your thumb, but quite possibly your future, your faith, your marriage, or your finances. It is a shaky world out there. But you have promises with which to face it. People of the Promise build their lives on the promises of God. When problems surface, they can be heard muttering, "But God said..." When struggles threaten, they can be seen flipping through Scripture, saying, "I think God said something about this." They make the deliberate choice to build their lives on promises of God, not the circumstances of life. They are like Abraham "who did not tiptoe around God's promise asking cautiously skeptical questions. He plunged into the promise and came up strong" (Romans 4:20 MSG).

As you trust the unbreakable promises, you discover God's unshakable hope.

As Scripture says:

We have this hope as an _____ for the _____, firm and secure. It enters the inner sanctuary behind the curtain, where our forerunner, _____, has entered on our behalf (Hebrews 6:19-20 NIV).

Look at the key terms of the first phrase: anchor and soul.

The anchor has one purpose—to steady the boat. You need an anchor like the tattoo on Popeye's forearm: heavy, castiron, and double pointed.

Why? Because you have a valuable vessel. You have a soul. An eternal being. The soul is that part of you that separates you from animals and unites you to God. And that soul needs an anchor.

Our anchor is set in the very throne-room of God. It will never break free. The anchor is set and the rope is strong. Why? Because it is beyond the reach of the devil and under the care of Christ.

Since no one can take your Christ, no one can take your hope.

Can death take your hope? No, because Jesus is greater than death. Can failure take your hope? No, because Jesus is greater than your sin. Can betrayal take your hope? No, because Jesus will never leave you. Can sickness take your hope? No, because God has promised—whether on this side of the grave or the other—to heal you. Death, failure, betrayal, sickness, and disappointment—they cannot take your hope, because they cannot take your Jesus.

I love how Hebrews 6:17–20 in the Message version puts it: "Just grab the promised hope with both hands and never let go. It is an unbreakable spiritual lifeline, reaching past all appearances to the very presence of God where Jesus, running on ahead of us, has taken up his permanent post as high priest for us."

Ask yourself this question: "Is what I am hooked to stronger than what I will go through?"

Everyone is anchored to something. Some are anchored to a retirement account, others to a resume. Some are tethered to a person; still others are attached to a position. "When the storm comes," they say, "this anchor will get me through."

Problem is, many of these folks are anchored to surface objects. You wouldn't do that in a boat, would you? Would you anchor to a buoy or another boat? Heaven forbid. You want something that goes deeper and holds firmer than other floating vessels. But when you anchor to things of this world are you not doing the same? Can a retirement account survive a depression? Can good health weather a disease? There is no guarantee.

Salty sailors would urge you to hook in to something solid. Hebrews gives you the same message. Do not trust the buoy on the water, do not trust the sailors in the next boat, and do not trust the other boat. In fact, do not even trust your own boat. When the storm hits, put your trust in no one but God.

Russell Kelso Carter did this. He was a star athlete and a top student. At the age of fifteen, during a prayer meeting, he surrendered his life to Christ. He later became an instructor at the Pennsylvania Military Academy and led a diverse and fruitful life that included stints as a minister, medical doctor, and even a songwriter. But it was his understanding of God's promises that makes his story relevant to us today.

Diagnosed with a critical heart condition by age thirty, Carter was facing imminent death. What did he do? He knelt and made a promise. Regardless of whether he got a healing or not, his life would be forever consecrated to the service of the Lord. From that moment on, the Scriptures in the Bible took on new life for Carter and he began to lean on the promises that he found there.

God chose to heal him and Carter lived, with a healthy heart, for another forty-nine-years. His decision to trust God in the midst of difficulties gave birth to a hymn that is still sung today.

The chorus goes....

Standing, standing,

Standing on the promises of God my Savior; Standing, standing,

I am standing on the promises of God

My favorite stanza in found in the second verse. It goes:

Standing on the promises that cannot fail,

When the howling storms of doubt and fear assail,

By the living Word of God I shall prevail,

Standing on the promises of God.

Do the same. Build your life on the promises of God. Since His promises are unbreakable, your hope will be unshakable. The winds will still blow. The rain will still fall. But, in the end, you will be standing, standing on the promises of God.

We are People of the Promise, and on His promises we will stand with unshakable hope.